Language and Translation

Theory, Pedagogy and Practice

Hilda Kebeya, Miriam Osore, Pamela Ngugi,
and Charles Kebaya (Editors)

Copyright © June 2016 Nsemia Inc. Publishers
All rights reserved.

This publication may not be reproduced, in whole or in part, by any means including photocopying or any information storage or retrieval system, without the specific and prior written permission of the publisher.

This book is sold subject to the condition that it shall not, by way of trade or otherwise, be re-sold, hired out, or otherwise circulated without the author's or publisher's prior consent in any form of binding or cover other than that in which it is published and without a similar condition including this condition being imposed on the subsequent purchaser.

First Edition: June 2016
Published by Nsemia Inc. Publishers (www.nsemia.com)

Edited By: Stella Riunga
Cover Concept & Design: Kemunto Matunda
Layout Design: Cyrus Kioko
Production Consultant: Matunda Nyanchama

Note for Librarians:
A cataloguing record for this book is available from Library and Archives Canada.

ISBN: 978-1-926906-47-8

Dedication

To educators, practitioners, students, and lovers of Language and Translation, we do hope that this gift will, in a little way, slake your thirst for knowledge in this field

Acknowledgements

A book of this magnitude does not easily come about unless there are people ready to sacrifice and devote their time, resources and intellectual abilities to make it happen. For this reason, we, the editors, are greatly indebted to a number of people who have significantly contributed to the realization of this book.

We thank the individual authors in this volume for painstakingly taking their time to write their chapters, revise them several times and most importantly, patently waited for this book.

To all our peer reviewers, we salute you for a job well done. Without you, we could not have ensured that the individual chapters herein meet the requisite threshold for publication. Thanks a million.

Table of Contents

Dedication - iii
Acknowledgements - v
Foreword........ix

Chapter One - 1
Translation Aesthetics: Reading Texts And Contexts in Ngugi's Caitaani Mutharaba-Ini And Devil On The Cross
Mugo Muhia and Macharia Mwangi

Chapter Two - 21
Hypertextuality And The African Literary Art: The Place Of Translation -
Eric C. Maritim

Chapter Three - 31
African Images In Kenyan Film As A Response To Colonial "Misrepresentations"
Rachael Diang'a and Oluoch Obura

Chapter Four - 59
Translation and Language Teaching
Amateshe S. Margaret

Chapter Five - 71
Translation In French Language Teaching and Learning
Velma Muyela

Chapter Six - 79
Interpretation In Judicial Settings
Gatitu Kiguru, Emily A. Ogutu and Martin C. Njoroge

Chapter Seven - 103
Translation in a Globalized World
Catherine Waithera Ndung'u

Chapter Eight - 115
Lexical Ambiguity of Homonymy and Polysemy in Ekegusii
Solomon Onchoke Aunga

Chapter Nine - 131
Translation Constraints in Media Advertisements Translated from English to Ekegusii
Samuel Komenda and Colleta Maniga

Notes on Contributors - 145

Foreword

Translation, both commercial and literary, is an activity that is growing phenomenally in today's globalized world (Bassnett, 2002). The study of translation, an interdisciplinary field known as Translation Studies, has also developed enormously in the past twenty years. It interfaces with a wide range of other disciplines from linguistics and modern languages to Cultural Studies and Post colonialism. This book attempts to investigate both the practice and theory of translation in an accessible and systematic way. It specifically explores the interfaces between theory, pedagogy and practice in the translation processes.

Throughout history, written and spoken translations have played a crucial role in inter human communication. The practice of translation, for instance, was crucial for the early dissemination of key cultural and religious texts and concepts. Eugene Nida (1998:12-23) places the beginning of translation with the production of the *Septuagint* which seems to have been the first translation of the Hebrew Old Testament into Greek. Once seen as a sub-branch of linguistics, translation today is perceived as an inter-disciplinary field of study and the indissoluble connection between language and way of life. Pioneer works in translation of scholars such as Mona Baker, J.C Catford, Michael Halliday, Roger Bell, Basil Hatim, Peter Newmark Kirsten Malmkjaer, Katharina Reiss, and Eugene Nida, to name but some of the better known, not only attest to this observation but also form a critical dynamic for subsequent research in Translation Studies.

Translation has a crucial role to play in aiding understanding of an increasingly fragmentary world. The translator, Michael Cronin has pointed out, is also a traveller, someone engaged in a journey from one source to another (Cronin, 2000). Significantly, a major development in Translation Studies since its beginning in the 1970s has been research into the history of translation, an examination of how translation has helped shape our knowledge of the world in the past better equips us to shape our own futures. This book has been born out of the need for further investigation of phenomenon of translation in theory, pedagogy and in practice. As this volume demonstrates, translation is classifiable into various categories. It can be divided into two general categories of literary and non-literary translation or the categories of ideational (technical and non-technical) and interpersonal (non-fictional and fictional) translation (Munday, 2008 & House, 1977), and the translation of pragmatic texts and literary or artistic texts (Basssnett, 2000 & Delisle 1988).

Of all the forms that translation takes, literary translation lets one consistently share in the creative process. Here alone does the translator experience the aesthetic joys of working with great literature, of recreating in a new language a work that would otherwise remain beyond reach. Literary studies have thus moved to what Peter France (2000), observes as "to tease out the different possibilities open to the translator, and the way these change according to the historical, social, and cultural context" (pg. 3). Mugo Muhia and Macharia Mwangi take a cue from this observation in their chapter, **Translation Aesthetics: Reading Texts and Contexts in Ngugi's *Caitaani Mutharaba-Ini* and *Devil on the Cross*.** In the chapter, the two authors show how specific linguistic choices in *Caitaani Mutharaba-ini* have profound aesthetic effects on an audience that is conversant with the Gikuyu idiom and how these have been impacted by translation. Whereas the reader of the original fully grasps the way meaning arises in certain allusions in the text, the reader of the translation may have to grapple with them. This is why the author who is also the translator has altered some linguistic choices in the translation and thereby curtailed the overall aesthetic actualization of the text. It has often been argued that grace, beauty, colour and flavour must be captured in literary translations and the resulting work must also be capable of being understood by its new audience, and make sense on every level (Paul, 2009). In this chapter, Mugo and Macharia implicitly posit important questions about how translation shapes a particular literary canon - ranging from translation strategies, norms in operation at a given point in time to measuring the impact and ethics of translation in literary studies.

Perhaps the most exciting new trend of all is the expansion of the discipline of Translation Studies is the electronic media explosion of the 1990s and its implications in intercultural communication. Electronic media has not only become an important space to access more of the world through the information revolution, but it has become an important site to understand one's own agency and point of departure in society. Indeed Eric Maritim aptly captures this state of affairs in **Hypertextuality and The African Literary Art: The Place of Translation**. The chapter extrapolates the place of translation in the light of the ever-expanding media spaces, especially on the cyberspace. It observes that the process of translation is perpetual and that at any given period of time, there is an imperative for some form of the translation process to be deployed. Such situation arises from the development of alternative socio-cultural realities afforded by the emergence and burgeoning of the World Wide Web and the attendant virtual space, commonly referred to as the cyberspace. Whereas the (de) colonized African subject endeavours to inscribe themselves into the (de)colonized spaces, Maritim attempts a prognosis of the translation of the African social imaginaries into the cyberspace which is overdetermined by the (Western) capital that lay claim to the cyberspace platforms.

The synergies between Film Studies and Translation Studies have been captured by Rachael Diang'a and Oluoch Obura in **African Images in Kenyan Film as a response to colonial "misrepresentations"**. Undeniably, the chapter is remarkably unique in the sense it focuses on Audiovisual translation in translation scholarship. Audiovisual translation, then, is a modality of translation which arose in the 1930s and it could be defined as the technical method that made the linguistic transfer of an audiovisual text possible. When talking about audiovisual translation, one must also take into account the technical procedure used in order to carry out the linguistic transfer from an audiovisual language to another (Chaume, 2004: 31). Dianga and Obura give the reader a flavour of the particularities of translating and interpreting films from a more descriptive perspective. The two propose a fair typology of transfer options in interpreting the (mis)representations of African images in cultural artefacts such as film. Importantly, their approach systematically takes into account that language(s) in films work(s) in tandem with non-verbal cinematic signifiers to create meaning.

The question of how translation and interpretation can be taught within the curricula of language studies remains a central concern among scholars of Translation studies. Margaret Amateshe in **Translation and Language Teaching** and Velma Muyela in **Translation in French Language Teaching and Learning** tackle issues of teaching and learning translation in a classroom system. In their respective chapters, the two explore competences required in teaching translation, and the elements of translation that can be developed through practice and those that require continual coaching. The two scholars also talk about the challenges and solutions in translation and interpreting within a classroom set up by combining theory and practice, hence allowing for implementation of the different methods of translation in real-life situations.

Legal translation is a special and specialised area of translation. Prominently, the complexity and difficulty of legal translation is attributable to the nature of law and the language that law uses, and the associated differences found in intercultural, interlingual and crosslinguistic communication in translating legal texts. Often, legal language is identified and linked with the normative, performative and technical nature of language use, and the inherent indeterminate nature of language in general. Amidst this complexity, Gatitu Kiguru, Emily A. Ogutu and Martin C. Njoroge's chapter **Interpretation in Judicial Settings** focuses on collocations and errors in legal translation. While focusing on the practice of translation and interpretation in the Kenyan court system, the chapter elaborates on the legal, linguistic and cultural complications as major sources of difficulty in legal translation. The chapter concludes by offering possible ways of mitigating these difficulties to ensure quality translations within the courtroom system.

Increased globalisation and widespread immigration have made readers more aware of cultural anomalies and more open to fresh ideas, different insights, and alternative developments. Catherinen Waithera Ndung'o in **Translation in a Globalized World** explores translation interlingual and intersemiotic translation in the globalized world as it relates to media, communication, culture and conflict. In her chapter, Ndung'o observes that globalization has led to a refreshing surge in interest in the unusual, diverse cultures and concerns. Through globalization, a whole new world has opened up, and the process of feeding this demand requires a stealthy and well-considered translation practice. Translators are an essential link in society to carry out businesses at the global stage.

Ambiguity is a pervasive phenomenon in human languages. It is not very hard to find words that are, to say the least, two ways ambiguous, or sentences which are grammatically correct but ambiguous in several ways. This is not only problematic because some of the alternatives are unintended (i.e. represent wrong interpretations), but because ambiguities 'multiply'. Ambiguities arising from translation processes witnessed across intercultural and interlingual communication are painstakingly interrogated in **Lexical Ambiguity of Homonymy and Polysemy in Ekegusii**. In this chapter, Onchoke S. Aunga identifies and analyzes homonymous and polysemous sense relations in Ekegusii language. Whilst analyzing the polysemous nature of Ekegusii, a characterisation of the language in terms of legal lexicon, syntax, pragmatics and style is done. The chapter concludes by examining how different types of linguistic and non-linguistic knowledge are necessary to resolve problems of ambiguity in translation.

Translating advertisements is no easy task for they are "a microcosm of almost all the prosodic, pragmatic, syntactic, textual, semiotic and even ludic difficulties to be encountered in translating" (Smith and Klein-Braley 1997: 175). However, in **Translation Constraints in Media Advertisements Translated from English to Ekegusii**, Samuel Komenda and Colleta Maniga embark on this taunting task showing how translated adverts can be read as "contact zones" where an interaction between "foreign" and "native" elements in these translated adverts can be explored. In the chapter, the taxonomy of rhetorical figures employed in the adverts is constructed and their translation investigated. The visibility of the linguistic Other is examined with reference to loanwords, loan meanings, and word formations. Eventually, while focusing on media adverts translated from English to Ekegusii language, the two scholars explore translation constraints in translating media adverts from one language to another and try to offer possible solutions to mitigate such constraints.

By and large, through a series of case analyses, writers in this volume have demonstrated a shift of emphasis that views translation as an act of creative rewriting to that of the translator, as an integral individual in translation processes. The primacy of the translator is underscored as someone who visibly endeavours to bridge the space between source author and text and the eventual target language readership. Indeed, this text celebrates a multidisciplinary approach to Translation Studies by combining experts, theoretical frameworks and methodologies from an impressively wide variety of academic fields, such as Linguistics, Literary Theory, Film Studies, Cultural Studies, New Media, Communication Studies, and Advertising, to mention but a few. The book presents and explores the intersections between theory, pedagogy and practice in Translation Studies, but these concepts can only be properly extended by careful pursuit of further reading and research in this area.

Dr. Waveney Olembo,
Senior Lecturer,
Department of Literature,
Kenyatta University.

References

Baker, Mona. (2006). *Translation and Conflict: A Narrative Account.* London/ New York: Routledge

----. (1998) *The Routledge Encyclopaedia of Translation Studies.* London and New York: Routledge.

Chäffner, Christina and Bassnett, Susan (eds) .(2011). *Political Discourse, Media and Translation.* Newcastle: Cambridge Scholars Publishing.

Chaume, Frederic. (2004). *Cine y traducción,* Cátedra, Madrid.

Cronin, Michael. (2000). *Across the Lines: Travel, Language, Translation.* Cork: Cork University Press.

Crystal, David. (2003). *A Dictionary of Linguistics and Phonetics.* Oxford: Blackwell.

Desilla, Louisa. (2014). "Reading between the lines, seeing beyond the images: An empirical study on the comprehension of implicit film dialogue meaning across cultures." The Translator 20(2). http://dx.doi.org/10.1080/13556509.2014.967476

France, Peter. (2000). *The Oxford Guide to Literature in English Translation.* Oxford: Oxford University Press.

Holmes, James S. (2004). The Name and Nature of Translation Studies. In Lawrence Venuti (ed.) (2004), The Translation Studies Reader, 2nd edition, pp. 180–92.

Jakobson, Roman. (2004). On Linguistic Aspects of Translation. In Lawrence Venuti (ed.) (2004), The Translation Studies Reader, 2nd Edition, pp. 138–43.

Munday, Jeremy. (2008): *Introducing Translation Studies*, New York: Routledge.

----. (2001). *Introducing Translation Studies: Theories and applications*, London and New York: Routledge.

Nord, Christiane. (2005). *Text Analysis in Translation: Theory, Methodology and Didactic Application of a Model for Translation-Oriented Text Analysis.* Amsterdam /Atlanta: Rodopi.

Nornes, Abe M. (2007). *Cinema Babel: Translating Global Cinema.* Minneapolis, MN: University of Minesota Press.

O'Sullivan, Carol. (2011). *Translating Popular Film.* Basingstoke: Palgrave MacMillan.

Paul, I. Gill. (2009). *Translation in Practice.* Champaign and London: Dalkey Archive Press

Pérez-González, Luis. (2014). *Audiovisual Translation: Theories, Methods and Issues.* Oxon: Routledge.

Shuttleworth, Mark & Cowie Moira. (1997). *Dictionary of Translation Studies*, Manchester: St Jerome.

Snell-Hornby, Mary. (2006). The Turns of Translation Studies. Amsterdam and Philadelphia: John Benjamins.

van Doorslaer, Luc. (2007). Risking Conceptual Maps. In Yves Gambier and Luc van Doorslaer (eds) The Metalanguage of Translation, special issue of Target 19. (2): 217–33.

Venuti, Lawrence (ed.) (2000). *The Translation Studies Reader.* London and New York: Routledge.

Chapter One
Translation Aesthetics: Reading Texts and Contexts in Ngugi's Caitaani Mutharaba-ini and the Devil on the Cross

Mugo Muhia and Mwangi Macharia

Introduction

The traditional conceptualisation of translation, as "faithlessness and betrayal of the original", has changed to that of a "bridge-building across the space between the source and target" and a "celebration of in-betweenness" of 21st century's borderless communities where "political, geographical and cultural boundaries are perceived as more fluid and less constraining than any time in recent history and the movement of people across those boundaries is increasing" (Bassnett:10-11). With these changes the role of the translator has come to be seen as that of "a liberator, someone who frees the text from the fixed signs of its original shape making it is no longer subordinate to the source text but visibly endeavouring to bridge the space between the source author and text and the eventual target language readership," ((Bassnett: 6). It has therefore come to be seen as a valuable process through which the text's life span is not only prolonged but people of different cultures converse and share ideas.

But even when the above is true, it is also true to point that translation in some instances has led to distortions, omissions and sometimes repression of particular issues and has in other cases deviated from cultural and social conditions which these texts have been produced. This chapter takes a view that a good translation must be based on a thorough understanding of the text's social, historical and cultural context in line with Foucault's view that "all knowledge is rooted in a life, a society, and a language that has a history; and it is in that very history that knowledge finds the element enabling it to communicate with other forms of life, other types of society, other signification," (372). The viability of translation depends on its relationship with cultural and social conditions surrounding its production. Ashok and Murray explain that the problem of translation is at times not related to language but "considerations which include the economics of publishing...This means that elements of neo-colonial relationship must inevitably enter the process of translation, since the balance of material and cultural power tends to lie with the former colonizers" (3). It remains a fact, therefore that there are certain nuances and connotations in the linguistics elements of a language that are bound to be lost or abstracted during translation.

In the translation of the Bible from English to Gĩkũyũ, for example the latter language lacked the equivalent term for Satan but within the Gĩkũyũ traditional religious belief system the manifestation of evil was discussed in the frame of the spirits what was referred to as "ngoma" with adjectives holy "njega" or good, and evil "njũru" or bad used to distinguish between the two types of spirits. The evil/bad spirits were believed to perturb people at will and therefore they were massaged by use of libations as a way of appeasing them. The Christian missionaries saw this as an evil practice meant at placating the devil and therefore in their translation of the term Satan collapsed the term "ngoma" to mean Satan and with time the term has come to connote evil in all its manifestation completely eclipsing it original meaning (Peterson, 2000: 143-45). This example shows how translation can at times change and completely alter the meaning of words and especially because of the ideology behind particular translations. Bassnett(4) supports this view when she points out that "translation can become submission to the hegemonic power of images created by the target culture."

This chapter therefore proceeds to show how specific linguistic choices in *Caitaani Mutharaba-ini* have profound aesthetic effects on an audience that is conversant with the Gikuyu idiom and how these have been watered down in the translation. Whereas the reader of the original fully grasps the way meaning arises in certain allusions in the text, the reader of the translation may have to grapple with them. This is why the author who is also the translator has altered some linguistic choices in the translation and thereby curtailed the overall aesthetic actualization of the text. We have restricted ourselves to oral literature genres, which we refer using the term orality – which was coined by Walter Ong and is currently used to refer to all expressive arts and to avoid the semantic ambiguity brought by the phrase oral literature – and the impact that translation has had on them. Orality is according to Ngugi (1986:95) a central feature in our appreciation of African literature. It is important therefore to interrogate what the reader of the original text gains aesthetically at the expense of the translated text's reader.

The comparative analysis between the Gikuyu text and its English translation also goes out to show, as Bell's puts it, that "The translator can only convey across the gulf of language the dross in a poem but inevitably loses the gold, though he may substitute for new gold of his own smelting... the simple transference of any poem form one tongue to another, as we might carry a vase of flowers from one room to another is forever impossible" (23). Bell's point is that a translated version of a text cannot entirely capture the aesthetic nuances of its original.

Elements of Oral Literature

In explaining the contextual nature of proverbs, Kabira and Mutahi have recounted a well-known Gikuyu anecdote:

Muhoro was a very mean person. One time there were people who planned to go and steal his cattle, goats and sheep. Somebody was sent to go and warn him about the plan. When this old man came to Muhoro's house, he sat down as was expected of him and waited for a while before giving the message; Muhoro asked the wives half-heartedly to give the old man something to eat. The women realizing that their husband was not serious did not give the man food. The man never gave Muhoro the message because he was disappointed. Muhoro was therefore caught unawares and his property was taken away – hence the proverb, *Kwa Muhoro gwakwire ngaguro* (Muhoro's home and wealth was destroyed because he and his wives could not give his messenger a welcoming token meal. (37)

The two have argued that proverbs emerge from specific settings within a given community; that once these proverbs are in use in the society, they are used to refer to similar kinds of situations. Thus they have concluded: "Proverbs are very culturally bound and therefore one has to understand the cultural contexts in order to fully appreciate their meaning and function," (38). This observation reinforces our view that there are certain aspects of the use of a language that are best appreciated by the reader/listener who is well versed with socio-cultural milieu of that language. This is particularly so in the literary use of language, particularly so where the application in question is that of oral literature genres. We seek to establish their aesthetic contribution to the story by virtue of their attribution to the idiom and the culture of the Gikuyu language speakers.

The central premise in this chapter is the fact that *Caitaani Mutharabaini* is a novel that is conceived and rendered in the framework of an oral narrative. This is a fact that Ngugi in *Decolonising the Mind* acknowledges when he says that he borrowed a lot from the oral tradition (78). It is therefore expedient for us to look at narration in the context of this tradition. Basically, narration refers to the way a story is developed through the manipulation of linguistic and extra-linguistic elements from the beginning to a meaningful end. In addition, given the centrality of performance in oral literature, it is fascinating to contemplate the novel as a performance by virtue of firstly, its being in part a quintessential parody of an actual rendition of an oral narrative and secondly, its being replete with elements of a Gicaandi performance.

In *Caitaani Mutharaba-ini*, there are implicit and explicit features of oral narration as a multi-generic creative process where the artists parade their wealth of knowledge on the idiom and the lore of their people. Besides the mastery of the plot, the artist embellishes the story through such stylistic choices as the proverbs, popular sayings, epigrams, songs and jokes. These are elements that abound in our text. Besides, oral narration is performed art. In the novel we have elements of oral performance including implied dramatization, particularly the use of implied gestures. Moreover, it is evident that the "I" narrator in the story addresses himself directly to an imaginary audience with which he strives to strike rapport and make an active participant in the delivery of the story. In fact the title *Muini wa Gicaandi* (The Gicaandi Player) is Ngugi's pet name for the story teller in this novel. We can take a closer look at some of the above elements.

Right from the beginning of the story, we get the impression that this is indeed an oral narrative. Like the normal Gikuyu oral fictional narratives, the narrator starts the novel with the opening formula, "*Uga itha*" (say *itha*). This is a statement that usually comes at the beginning of a Gikuyu oral narrative to alert the audience and as Kabira and Mutahi have shown, "is a clear indicator that the artist is taking you into a fictional world" (6). This formula and introductory remarks are left out in the translation.

Still in the introductory part, the narrator animatedly invokes the presence of a listener to whom he beckons in the words "*uka muraata/ uka twaranirie!/ uka twaranirie riu!/uka twaranitire cie Jacinta Wariinga utaanatua ciira wa ciana ciitu..*" (CM 3) (come, my friend/come and let us reason together now/come and let us reason together about Jacinta Wariinga before you pass judgement on our children..." (DC 9). The whole narrative is thus presented as an attempt to put the facts about Wariinga in the right so that the friend (audience) may make a fair judgment of her. This is made more concrete by the use of the collective "we" narrative voice implying the audience/reader is indeed actively present in the narration. A perfect example is at the introduction of the main story, the second part where the narrator requests to start the story a fresh: "*Hi! Anga ni ndaarugirira rugano. Mathiina ma Wariinga matiambiriiriea Ilmorog. Reke turutie uhoro mbara Nginyo...*" (CM 4) ("Wait!") I am leaping ahead of the story. Wariinga's troubles did not begin at Ilmorog. Let us retrace our steps... ") (DC 10). The exclamation "Hi!" ("Wait!") presumes an addressee who is physically present at the site of the utterance. And the statement "Let us retrace our steps..." is quite revealing of what we need not overemphasize here: the narrator and the narrattee are both actively involved in the process of the narration of the story of Wariinga.

Performance means dramatization. Besides, hardly can any form of enactment be devoid of gestures. And as we delve deep into Caitaani, we occasionally discern certain linguistic choices that suggest drama, that conjure in our minds gestures used by the narrator. We can cite a few of these. The first example is in Wariinga's anecdote where Kareendi is made to wait for her boss after normal working hours. As she waits anxiously the narrator marks the passage of time as follows:

> *Thaa ikumi na imwe ni ici. Boss Kihara hihi ari gwake wabici agicora marua. Thinaacara ino.* (CM 15)

> Five o'clock. Boss Kihara is in his office drafting the letters, perhaps. Six o'clock. (DC 21).

The expression of time in the vernacular text is done with implied gestures suggesting the arrival of time. The more literal translation of the phrases of time used in the original would be "Five o'clock is this" and "Here is six o'clock. The use of the demonstrative pronoun 'this' and the adverb 'here' suggests action. These are done away with in the translation. A similar example is where Mukiraai says about his moving from the University of Nairobi to America: He puts it as "*Nii nii ucio. O America...*" (CM 72). Translated as "Then, forward march. In America...." (DC 77). The Gikuyu statement, which we could also translate as "Then there I go. To America..." not only suggest a variation in the tone of the speaker but also a probable accompanying gesture or facial expression that would demonstrate the concept of the great leap in space by the speaker, moving from Kenya to America.

That the narrative persona is actively conscious of his "audience" close at hand is again demonstrated as the story gathers speed towards its momentous climactic end. This is at the beginning of Part Ten where the story teller agonizes aloud, sharing his doubts and anxieties with his 'friend' whose opinion he seeks and whom he urges to keep on giving him company:

> *Ngwambiriria ha? Kana hihi ndige kuhithuria hitho ciene?.... No ningi ri, ndaari Kuu Naikuru iyo iganagwo. Ni ndeeyooneire na maya, ngigwira na maya.... Giuke muraata... Uka o riu.... Uka tuthii naawe ngugererie tucira turia Wariinga aagererie, uka tumuume makinya thuutha tukionaga na maitho maitu ma ngoro kiria oonaga, tukiiguaga na matu maitu ma ngoro kiria Wariinga aiguuaga, geetha tutikaahiuhe kumutuira ciira na uira wa njuuku.*(CM 218)

Where shall I begin? Or should I stop involving myself in other people's lives? But I too was present in Nakuru. I saw with my own eyes and heard with my ears.... So, come, my friend, come with me so I can take you along the paths that Wariinga walked. Come let us retrace her footsteps, seeing with the eyes of our hearts what she saw, and hearing with the ears of our hearts what she heard, so that we shall not be hasty in passing judgment on the basis of rumour and malice. (DC 215)

To begin with, the rhetorical questions that are ideally directed towards the friend/ audience (reader) have been used to achieve both rhythm and suspense. Rhythm is especially reinforced by the fact that the passage cited constitutes very short sentences partly patterned in verse form. Secondly, dramatization is again experienced in the vernacular text like where the narrater says, "*ndeeyooneire na maya na ngiigwira na maya*" (I saw for myself with these ones and heard for myself with these ones). The demonstrative pronoun 'these' is an implied gesture used to point at the narrater's eye and ears respectively (which explains why the two pairs of organs are not mentioned in the Gikuyu text). The translation, which leaves out the nuances of oral performance we experience in the original, has had to mention them: "I saw with my own eyes and heard with my ears". Moreover, the narrator solicits the company of the listener(s) explaining that they have to continue the story together for it is the quest through which they will arrive at a sound judgment of Wariinga. These strategies cultivate a strong rapport between the narrator and the audience/reader.

The other feature of oral literature that is extensively used as a narrative strategy in the novel is oral poetry. The use of songs and other forms of oral poetry is a practice that traditionally accompanied most cultural events in African societies. Consequently, African oral poetry was for many years deemed to be merely a functional, ritualistic enactment during specific ceremonies. It was hardly appreciated as an art form. But later scholars--notably Ruth Finnegan, Okpewho Dathorne, and Wanjiku Kabira, among others--have put up a strong case for the artistic input of individual performers in terms of creativity at the moment of delivery of the oral item.

It is certainly not for their ritualistic value that Ngugi appropriates oral poetry forms, including songs and recitations in *Caitaani Mutharaba-ini* and his other works. It is for their potential as literary forms of imaginative expression. It is for their contribution in terms of rhythm, the tempo of the story, in terms of creation of a suitable atmosphere, the right mood, in building up or relieving of suspense. Indeed, the use of songs and poems in the narrative situates it in the tradition of storytelling under the full moon where the narrator would occasionally break into a song, acquiring a firmer grip on the story line and the audience in the process.

It is these aesthetic qualities that Ngugi adeptly exploits to embellish the story of Wariinga. This is particularly effective in the vernacular text.

There are numerous other instances of the use of oral poetry in the novel. There is a panaroma of the sub-genres of songs including traditional types such us *irua, mwomboko* and *muthunguci*, religious songs, prayers and chants, patriotic and mobilization songs and even contemporary music such as the lingala songs spewed forth by the Hells Angels band at the cave in Ilmorog. Such a conglomeration of voices is what Gatuiria has been striving to assemble in his two years research into the history of Kenyan music and culture. The song motif, therefore, runs throughout the narrative. And it is not surprising that the braggadocio of thieves and robbers is idiomatically referred to as *kuina kaari* (to sing and dance *kaari*, that is, to sing and dance to one's self-praise). Indeed, the whole story is also conceived in the paradigm of an expansive song; sooled, as it were, by the Gicaandi player who nevertheless keeps on taking to the backstage to leave individual performers (characters) in the story to sing their set parts.

We start our analysis of oral poetry by looking at Gicaandi as a quaint art form that Ngugi has adapted, cannibalising and recasting it in this postmodern story where the ancient and the contemporary merge to complement each other, innovatively constructing this solid work that he would happily call 'the African novel'.

Gitahi Gititi has done an informative exegesis of Gicaandi highlighting its dialectical and multi-generic essence, and explaining how it is appropriated by the author in Devil on the_Cross. He has documented that virtually all the genres of oral literature coalesce in a Gicaandi text. "Even a cursory reading of a Gicaandi text reveals the complex interplay of genres- riddles, proverbs, biographical "information", history, commentary and a performative dramatic quality, which invest in voices, gesture and attention to the audience"(109). Yet in spite of Ngugi invoking Gicaandi in the person of the autobiographical narrator in the story, the novel may not really be considered akin to the Gicaandi performance per excellence. In explaining the nature of Gicaandi Fr. Cagnolo has written thus:

The singer of the Geshande... goes round the country... and stops on the markets and squares to sing his song to the accompaniment of bottle-gourd which he waves to and fro...He challenges any other singer to know as many verses as he does. In case he is defeated, he loses his instrument. The song may go on for a whole day. (166)

The performance is a kind of a game of wits which involves coding and decoding of messages that require quick thinking, vast knowledge of the life and experience of the Aagikuyu, and a sense of fair play. (Kabira and Mutahi, 33). In *Caitaani Mutharaba-ini* we can only identify features that are appropriated from *Gicaandi* both in form and content but we can neither consider Ngugi's "I" narrator as an exact copy of *Muini wa Gichandi* (singer of *Gicandi*) nor the story a perfect parody of a *Gicaandi* performance. The use of this art form should therefore be appreciated within the broader perspective of oral narration.

The other aspect that falls under the poetic forms in the novel is the use of verse. The novel is essentially written in prose. Incidents of verse in the traditional novel are few and are usually in form of actual or implied quotations. However, in <u>*Caitaani Mutharaba-ini*</u>, there are instances where prose melts into verse especially in some dramatic moments in the story. This is especially in the earlier parts of the story and towards the end where the *Gicaandi* Player gets lyrical, evidently strives to captivate the audience (reader).

In the introduction (Part one), for instance, where after seven days of fasting he is commandeered by the spirits to deliver the prophesy to the people, the Prophet of Justice submits, crying out:

Nii ndeetikira	I accept
Ni ndeetikira	I accept
Ngiria kiriro ngoro-ini	Silence the cries of the heart
Ngiria maithori ngoro-ini (CM2)	Wipe away the tears of the heart(DC 8)

The last (third) section is a blending of poetry and prose where the three single sentence paragraphs are punctuated with the lines announcing the narrator's acceptance, which creates a regular rhythm in a sort of an artistic tango (between verse and prose) culminating in the concluding dramatic recital:

> *Gwithaamba ni kuruta nguo*
>
> *Guthambira ni gutoboka rui*
>
> *Ni wega uguo...*
>
> *Uka*
>
> *Uka murata*
>
> *Uka twaranirie!*
>
> *Uka twaranirie riu!*
>
> *Uka twaranirie cia Jacinta Wariinga utaanatha cira wa ciana ciitu...   (CM3).*

To bathe is to strip off all clothes

To swim is to plunge into the river

Come

Come my friend

Come let us reason together now

Come and let us reason together about

Jacinta Wariinga before you pass judgment on our children...
(DC9)

The basic difference between the original and the translation is that the words in the Gikuyu text are more compact and more charged with emotion than in the English one. The sound patterns are more elaborate in *Caitaani Mutharaba-ini* than in *Devil on the Cross* like, for example, in the first illustration where *ngiria* means both 'silence' and 'wipe away' and alliterates with *ngoro-ini*, which is not the same for 'silence' and wipe away-- they can never alliterate with 'of the heart'.

Similarly, in the case of the second illustration, it starts with a pair of proverbs whose wording enhances the musicality of the verse. The near semblance, for instance, of the orthographic/enunciatory nature of their first words *gwithaamba* (to bathe) and *guthambira* (to swim) is a good case in point. Moreover, the flow of verse is something a kin to a chain song. Therefore the Gikuyu versions are inevitably much more sonorous than their translations.

Another classic example is the *marebeta* (poems) that are used by the university student as he cautions Wariinga about life in Nairobi:

Nairobi ino riu,	Today Nairobi teaches
Ithiinguraga muthingu	Crookedness to the kind,
Igatugura mutugi	Meanness to the kind,
Ikeendithukia mwendani	Hatred to the loving,
Ikeegu kia mwega	Evil to the good,
(CM 10)	(DC 16)

This poem is an enactment of the struggle between good and evil. The author uses poetic license to coin fresh verbs, which helps him to achieve profound poetic effects in terms of sound, rhythm and cryptic juxtaposition of theses and antitheses. Perhaps an unconventional translation of the above would shed more light on this:

This Nairobi today,

Unholies the holy

Unkindens the kind

Unlovens the loving

Ungoodens the good

Our translation may strike us as crude. But in the original text it is nothing but novel. In either case the message is clear: Nairobi is a dehumanizing city.

As we mentioned at the beginning of the chapter proverbs are the other genre of oral literature whose meaning and aesthetic function is to some extent socially and culturally determined. The place and significant of proverbs in African oral tradition is perhaps best articulated by Chinua Achebe in *Things Fall Apart* where the narrator says:

Having spoken *plainly* so far, Okoye said the next half a dozen sentences in proverbs. Among the Ibo the *art of conversation* is regarded very highly, and proverbs are the *palm oil with which words are eaten.* Okoye was a great talker and he spoke for a long time, skirting round the subject and then hitting it finally. (5, emphasis mine)

In the first place, this observation seems to discredit *plain* language (like the one Okoye had used) and goes on to attribute the aesthetic quality in the *art of conversation* to the use of proverbs. The image the palm oil underpins the centrality of proverbial language to the enjoyment of speeches among the Ibos. Ruth Finnegan corroborates this fact in her observation about public speaking in Africa: "...aesthetic considerations are also involved, if only to add to the persuasiveness of the speech... we often hear of the use of proverbs on such occasions to appeal to the audience or make a point with extra forcefulness" (445). Not only are proverbs used to introduce an idea; they are also used to develop an argument (to *skirt round the subject* in Achebe's idiom). Besides, they often act as potent clinchers to an argument.

Ngugi has extensively appropriated the proverbial language of the speech of the Agikuyu community as a narrative technique. We are here using the term 'proverbial' in the broader sense of the word, which according to *Collins Concise Dictionary* means, "of, embodied in or resembling a proverb". We are as such going to address ourselves to popular idiomatic expressions, sayings and epigrams, and the proverbs themselves. The basic distinction that we give between 'popular discourse' and the 'proverbs' is that the popular is that which is commonly used among the general public and which is easily comprehensible as contrasted with the proverb which is usually more dense in terms of language use and content, and therefore tends to be a preserve of the experienced communicators, mostly the elders. This is what Finnegan alludes when she asserts:

It will emerge that, in addition to terseness and relative fixity, most sayings classed as proverbs are also marked by some kind of poetic quality in style or sense, and are in this way set apart in form from more straightforward maxims. (393)

Caitaani Mutharaba-ini is full of popular idiomatic expressions and sayings. For the sake of our analysis we are going to sample some of these. Adhering to the principle of self-preservation, there are times in the Gikuyu traditional value system when it is deemed prudent that you keep quiet about a truth that you know, lest you get yourself destroyed. This is what the *Gicaandi* Player invokes when he wonders: " *Nii ni nii u, kanua weriire?*" (CM 1) ("Who am I-the mouth that ate itself?") (DC, 7). The statement expresses the narrator's dilemma on whether to tell the story of Wariinga or not, bearing in mind the drastic repercussion it might bring him for provoking the wrath of the people in power. This same phrase is used by Mwaura who describes himself and other matatu taxi drivers as *kanua weriire* (42) for their being reckless word-mongers. This expression serves the same function as the proverbs: "*Kari guoya kainukiire nyina*" (The cowardly warrior went back safely to his mother) and "*Kwigita ti guoya*" (Shielding oneself is not cowardice). They all warn the individual against irresponsible bravado. Another interesting reference to the mouth and its speech habits is the expression *kanua moonjore*. The first word means 'the mouth' but the second one is hardly translatable. The phrase refers to a mouth that spews forth a lot of words, which may not be believed or trusted. In the novel, Wariinga quotes Kareendi in her anecdote as saying, "*O nanii ni ndaritukwo ndari icio cia kanua monjoore*" (CM 12) which is translated as "I have lost faith in silk tongued gigolos" (DC 18). Mwaura who hopes to win himself more passengers uses this again. He says: "*Ngigaakinya Rimuru ndahoota kuona akuo aingi... ndimatahe na kanua moonjore* " (CM 28), translated as, "Before I get to Limuru, I may find more passengers... and I can win them over with sweet words" (DC 34). The expression is epithetic and it underlines the community's high regard for honesty and sincerelity. In this sense, the original reader has a vast reservoir of choices within which to interpret and understand unlike the one of the translated version.

There are a host of other popular expressions of the Gikuyu language in the novel. For now it will suffice to look at one more example of the popular idiom in the text. This is phrase "*andu matoi i kana e* (CM 108) (people who do not know *i* or *e*). This is used by Kihaahu wa Gatheeca when he says how he decided to start his own school after observing that even illiterate people were starting schools and making a lot of money. The origin of this expression could be traced in the fact that

Language and Translation

when children go to school the first thing they do in the study of language are the vowels. The lower primary classrooms usually resonate with the chant of the vowels, a e i o u. Coming, as it were, as a song, it has so appealed to the imagination of the casual listener as to come up with the idiom *kumenya i kana e* (to know i or e) to refer to literacy. The translation in the English novel is "people who could hardly read or write A or B" (DC 111). Though it makes sense, especially when accompanied by the words 'read or write', and in spite of its being altered to consist of A and B, the idiom remains foreign to the English language to be as fully appreciated as the vernacular one.

Aphorisms and epigrams are the other aspects of proverbial language that we encounter in the popular culture of a people. *Longman Dictionary of Contemporary English* gives the meaning of an aphorism as a concise pithy saying that expresses a fact; an adage, and an epigram as a pointed witty statement often with a paradoxical twist. Janheinz Jahn on the other hand has quoted Doke as having observed the following about aphorism and by extension African oral literature:"A glance at the literary form of aphorism in any (Bantu) language makes it abundantly clear that they are different from ordinary prose utterances. The difference is not entirely due to the pithiness of the sayings, but also to a tendency towards the rhythmic, a tendency which at times borders on the poetic" (Jahn 58). He goes on to point out some of these poetic qualities as the parallelism in syntax, doubling of words, alliteration and rhymes. It need not be overemphasized that it is practically impossible to directly translate the rhythmic/poetic qualities of these statements from the original language to another. An analysis of a few of these in Caitaani will serve to illustrate this. A good example is when Wariinga says as she narrates the story of Kareendi. "*No bata ndubatabataga* " (CM 13). The translation of this only retains the content but is devoid of the poetic elements of the original: "But problems don't have wings to bear them away" (DC 18). The original is concise and expressive. It invests in onomatopoeia--the word *batabata* is the imitation of the sound made by the wings of a bird as it flies off. The statement means that you have to make an effort to solve a problem afflicting you for the problem cannot solve itself. But whereas the meaning of this aphorism is central to the development of the story, it is its rhythmic, its poetic nature that we relish as readers.

There is a series of similar popular sayings in the text whose literariness is experienced in its profundity, not in the message, but in the poetic quality that we experience in the Gikuyu version but lost in the translated one. One of these is the statement directed to Kareendi by her reneging boyfriend, Kamoongonye when he reprimands her, saying; "*Uracama ari njeme*" (CM 19), which is translated as "He who tastes develops a penchant for tasting" (DC 25). The other one is what Wangari says upon her decision not to say much in the matatu: "*Metumi Magunirwo ni gwituma*" (CM33), translated as "The people from the land of silence were once saved by silence " (DC 39). Thirdly there is the saying "*Rugendo in kugeenda*" (CM 39) translated as "Traveling is what makes a journey" (DC 36). Finally we have the epigram used by Mwaura as he touts for passengers: "*Munyaka niunyakukagwo*" (CM 29) which is translated as "Good fortune can change to ill fortune" (DC 34). These examples have one thing in common: in them thrives the interplay of sound and meaning, and the repetition of a word or part of the word, which contributes immensely to their rhythm. This is lost in the translations, which are in form of explanation, which has undone the terseness of the original and hence reduced their aesthetic potential.

The situation is not any different when we look at the more dense proverbs. Nevertheless, proverbs may not so much invest in the sound and rhythmic pattern a aphorisms and epigrams: the strength of proverbs lies in the metaphoric and symbolic language in which they are couched. This is what Finnegan notes when she says: "In many African cultures a feeling for language, for imagery and for the expression of abstract ideas through compressed and allusive phraseology comes particularly in proverbs"(390). And she quite aptly asserts that they are not isolated sayings on their own but "just one aspect of artistic expression within a whole social and literary context" (393). In the strength of these observations, we proceed to analyze a few proverbs in <u>Caitaani</u> within the context of the Aagikuyu language and culture.

In the lore of the Aagikuyu community the heart is usually taken to be analogous to a forest. Living in a region characteristic of the tropical forests of Africa, the community traditionally considered the forest as pivotal to the well being of its members: it is the life giving, life sustaining reservoir from which the springs and the rivers flow, providing water for life. Its flora and fauna fed the people by providing fruit and firewood for the former and meat for the later. In times of adversity, it served as a haven of retreat for safety. Is it then not quite congruous that the heart (which to the Aagikuyu is the essence of being,-- quite indistinguishable from the soul) is deemed akin to the forest insofar as in it resides the deepest secrets, fears, despairs, most cherished dreams, etc., that the individual may leash or unleash to secure his happiness, his survival or at his own peril? It is this contextual social matrix that the proverb,

"*Mutitu uri ngoro nduunagwo ngu igathira* (CM 1) (the forest in the heart is not cleared of all its firewood), should be appreciated. The proverb is used by, the Prophet of Justice, as he agonizes over whether or not in telling Wariinga's story he is not going to jeopardize his life.

This proverb is accompanied by another one before the narrator issues a concluding statement. This tendency to use a series of proverbs in a row is quite frequent in the story. This has contributed greatly to the tempo and the rhythm of the narrative. A look at the paragraph in which the above proverb falls illustrates this.

Nii o naanii murathi wa kihooto ni ndaambite kurituhirwo ni murigo uyu, njugage atiri: mutitu uri ngoro nduunagwo ngu igathira. Cia mucii ti como. Ilmorog ni gwitu. (CM 11)

I, even I, Prophet of Justice, felt this burden weigh heavily upon me at first, and I said: *the forest of the heart is never cleared of all its trees. The secrets of the homestead are not for the ears of strangers.* Ilmorog is our homestead. (DC7)

The proverbs in the original come as short terse statements which when arranged in a row and given their poetic diction form a rhythmic pattern that is captivating to the reader. This is considerably lost in translation where the equivalent in English often appears to be more like an explanation than a match for the original. The second proverb in the above paragraph, '*cia mucii ti como*' for example, is short alliterative and quite novel in its use of the word '<u>como</u>' (which is a corruption of the verb <u>comora</u> [pull out]). Its translation says the same but in a loose, uninteresting and mundane manner. The tempo in the paragraph is slowed down. This dulls the aesthetic sensation that is quite pointed in the original.

An outstanding example of the extensive use of proverbs in the story is where Gatuiria recounts how the old man from Bahati who narrated to him the story of Ndiguri started the story:

Aambiriirie na thimo gakuundi.... Akiuga: na toondu kwerirwo ati uthuri wa ndoonga dunuungaga, na ati ndoonga igiragio igaanjo na ikarima, muundu o wothe eekwendo amenyage ati wainaga in eeroragira, na waringaga ni atobokaaga. Woni we njaci, wagi gitaranio. Kwenda muno ni kwiyeendia. Mwananke uyu caria indo. No ndukaanonie Ngai nda, na ndukaanoonie Kiriindi matanuko. Mugaambo wa kirindi niguo mugaambo wa Ngai. (CM 58)

He started off with several proverbs....He told me that though it is said that the fart of a rich man has no smell, and that a rich man will cultivate even a forbidden, sacred shrine, still every man ought to know that he who used to dance can now only watch while others do it, and he who used to jump over the stream can now only walk through it. To possess much encourages conceit; to possess little, thought. Too much greed may well prompt one to sell oneself cheaply. "Young man," he said, "go after property. But never show God your nakedness and never despise the people. The voice of the people is thevoice of God. (DC 63)

This is a typical Gikuyu old man speaking, "skirting around the subject", giving the young listener some food for thought, and not without creating a great deal of suspense. In this particular incident, the knack of storytelling in the oral tradition is demonstrated where the storyteller introduces a story with a proverb, proverbs or the riddles to whet the enthusiasm of the audience.

Turning to riddling as a popular practice, which has been appropriated into our narrative avails us exciting insights as to how oral literature could further flavour the form of the novel. Granted, we have already referred to some riddles in the previous chapter in the light of figurative presentation. But this should not deprive us of the opportunity now to contemplate the riddle in the broader sense as a quaint art form among the Aagikuyu.

Having carried out a study on the general and linguistic structure of riddles in Bantu, P.D Beuchat has the following to say: "Most of the features of the linguistic structure of Bantu riddles to a great extent, cannot be translated into English. Symmetry of syllable patterns and onomatopoeic idiophones are culture-bound-or rather language-bound" (182). This is true of the few riddles that are used in *Caitaani Muthara-ini*. One of the riddles that has been elaborately appropriated is a popular riddle "*Ndathii uu, ndathii uu – njira cia ategi*. (I go this way I go that way – the hunters' path). The riddle is provoked by Wariinga's question to Muturi whether he would attend a devil's feast. Muturi says:

Gwata ndai ngugwati cia kiiriu "Ndaathii uu ndathii uu!" Muturi akiuga.

"Njira cia ategi," Wangari akiugira Wariinga.

"Aaca!"

"Oya kigacwa."

"Njira cia aturi! Gwata riingi!"

"Ndaagwata."

"Ndathii uu, ndathii uu!!"

"Njira cia aruti wira. Gwata o riingi."

Ndagwata

Ndathii uu ndoreete gwa ituika

Njira cia aruti a-wira

Language and Translation

"*ii, na aaca. Rehe kigacwa na ndigukugaca muno ni wamenyamenya.*"

"*Oya!*"

"*Njira cia aregi...... na no cio cia aruti-a-wira....*
(CM/66/67)

"Let me ask you a modern riddle....

"I walk this way and that way!" Muturi said

"The ways of hunters." Wangari answered for Wariinga

"No!"

"Take a forfeit!"

"The paths of builders! Answer another riddle"

"I will!"

"I walk this way and that way!"

"The paths of builders."

"No give me a forfeit."

"It's yours."

"The paths of workers. Answer another."

"I will!"

"I walk this way and that way towards a revolution."

"The paths of workers."

"Yes and no. You owe me a forfeit, but I won't take everything for you got half the answer."

"I accept that."

"The answer is the paths of resistance.... And those are the paths made by workers." (DC 71)

The riddle form contributes to the thematic development of the novel in an interesting way. Muturi who acts as the author's mouthpiece seizes the movement upon Wariinga's question to manipulate the lore of the people to underscore the role of workers in bringing about a revolution. Taking the nature of a question and answer dialogue between the poser (Muturi) and the respondent (Wangari), this exchange in the now innovated and extended riddle occasions a light moment in the text. It Is done playfully as we can, for instance, perceive in the asking for and giving of a forfeit between Muturi and Wangari. Significantly, this is yet another stylistic choice in the story where form in oral literature enhances the aesthetic function of the text.

Another genre of oral literature that abounds in *Caitaani Mutharaba-ini* is that of names and nicknames. "Names can be used as a succinct and oblique ways of commenting on their owners or on others," says Finnegan (470). She contends--as a host of other scholars of African Oral Literature have done--that names form an important part of oral literature in Africa. Several critics have talked about the literary significance of names in the works of Ngugi. They have established that names of characters especially in his later novels are deeply symbolic. In Caitaani, for instance, most of the names are emblematic of the character and worldview of the respective individuals given. The most striking of these are the names of 'the thieves and robbers', all of which serve to show their heinous nature. They designate different versions of exploitation such as Kahuria (snatcher), Gataanguru (tapeworm), Gatheeca (sucker) and Nguunji (squeezer). It is interesting to observe that the writer has used the augmentative and deminutive forms for the first and last names of Kahuria, Gatheeca and Gataanguru. This intensifies their bestiality. Besides they are humorous and grotesque. Their English names such as *Rotten Borough Ground Fresh Shitland Narrow Isthmus Joint Stock Brown (Gitutu wa Gataanguru – Jigger son of tapeworm)* complete the caricuture in the melodramatic moment in the narrative as the crooks horn their fame to the audience in the cave. The use of these names as satirical devices ridicules the men's greed for wealth and their vanity. That the Gikuyu names are not translated is an obvious loss for the reader of the English version.

An equally interesting aspect is the use of nicknames and epithets for some characters in the story. We have *Wariinga Marakara* (Wariinga the Angry One), *Mahua Kareendi* (Kareendi the flowers) *Kareendi ciero* (Kareendi of thighs) *Mahuthu Karekia* (The Easy to yield) and *Thaara wa Wainaina* (Napier-grass Son of Trembling) to mention a few. They intrigue us for their idiomatic presentation, which is not without a tinge of humour. There is more of playfulness than abhorrence in their use in spite of their being epithets of apparent condemnation. Just like the names above, the nicknames and epithets echo the Gikuyu popular folklore and are a great source of comic effect and satire. Whereas they appear as real (proper) names in their Gikuyu version, they seem to be mere descriptive phrases in translation.

Conclusion

The one thing that has propelled our investigation along in this chapter, as much as in the previous ones is the question: how does a writer of a literary text communicate for maximum aesthetic effect? We have throughout the chapter contended that aesthetics are more often than not inherent to an individual language and the lore of a people. Besides, oral literature has proved to be the very embodiment of what Dathorne calls the experience of a people "stored in the memory of a tribe", whereby, in his words again, the artist acts as "the link that bound art to the life of a people.... The continuous expression of living art" (7).

We have looked at the use of popular discourse as it is the case with popular idiomatic expressions, popular sayings, epigrams, aphorisms and proverbs, of which we have established that their aesthetic realization is not just in their witty or cryptic sense, but more so in their compactness, their diction, and the subsequent rhythmicality. We have looked at other short forms including the riddles, names and nicknames. We have also looked at the versified forms as derived from oral poetry. And we have sought to locate all the above in the tradition of oral narration. Thus we have concluded that *Caitaani Mutharaba-ini* could be conceived as an oral narration in which the narrator employs multi-generic narrative strategies to achieve a carnival of aesthetic effects in the text. The same cannot be said of its translated version.

We have also looked at language as a literary expression at the level of imaginative comparison and especially in the use of figurative language. Owing to the fact that figurative language derives its objects of comparison from a people's immediate environment, we have shown that there are a host of similes metaphors and instances of personification that demands that the reader be well versed with the language and the folklore of the Aagikuyu to fully comprehend certain allusions in the text. This has therefore attested that translation does in some instances limit our comprehension of texts because the language of translation has a different cultural convention and also because the images that inform it are different. The embellishment that figurative language gives the Gikuyu text is compromised in the translated text.

Finally, our comparative analysis of *Caaitani Mutharaba-ini* and *Devil on the Cross* has shown in each case the difference in terms of the aesthetic realization of the individual text. What has emerged from our investigation is not the superior language vis a vis the inferior language dichotomy. Rather, we have demonstrated that the two are, to some extent, different texts whereby by virtue of its being the original, *Caaitani Mutharaba-ini* has intrinsic aesthetic merits that have been lost in the translation.

Works Cited

Achebe, Chinua. Things Fall Apart. Nairobi: Heinemann, 1958.

Bassnett, S. Translation Studies. London and New York: Routledge, 2002.

Bell, H. Idvis, "The Problem of Translation" *Literature and life Addresses to the English   Association.* London: George H & Co., 1948. (9-28)

Beuchat, P.D., "Riddles in Bantu" The study of Folklore. Allan Dunde ed, London: Prentice Hall, 1965.

Cagnolo. C. *The Akikuyu: their customs, Traditions, and Folklore.* Nyeri: Catholic Mission of Consolata Fathers, 1933.

Dathorne O. *The Black Mind.* London: University of Minnesota Press, 1974.

Finnegan, Ruth. *Oral Literature in Africa.* Nairobi: Oxford University Press, 1970.

Gititi, Gitahi, "Recuperating a Disappearing Art Form: Resonance of 'Gicaandi' in *Devil On the Cross*", The World of Ngugi wa Thiongo, Charles Cantalupo, ed, New Jersey: Paintbrush, 1993. (109-127)

Jahn, Janheinz. *Neo-African Literature: A History of Black Writing.* New York: Grove Press Inc., 1968.

Kabira, Wanjiku, Karega wa Mutahi. *Gikuyu Oral Literature.* Nairobi: East African Educational Publishers, 1988.

Ngugi wa Thiongo. *Caitaani Mutharaba ini.* Nairobi: Heinemann, 1980.

_____ *Devil on the Cross.* Nairobi: East African Educational Publishers, 1982.

_____ *Decolonising the Mind: The Politics of Language in African Literature.* Nairobi: Heinemann, 1986.

Peterson, D. (2000(. *Writing Gikuyu: Christian Literacy and Ethnic Debate in Northern Central Kenya, 1908-1952.* Ph.D Thesis: University of Minnesota.

Chapter Two

Hypertextuality and the African Literary Art: The Place of Translation

Eric Maritim

Introduction

Statistics relating to access and use of the information technology, especially the internet, suggest a dismal narrative about African countries. Internet World Stats, for example, indicates that by 2013, Africa as a whole had an internet penetration of 21.3%, and the internet users in the continent constitute 8.6% of internet users worldwide (Internet World Stats). Europe alone has an internet penetration of 68.6% of its total population of slightly over 800 million. Internet users in this region account for 20.2% of users worldwide. In North America, the penetration is estimated to be 84.9% with this population of users constituting 10.7% of the users worldwide.

Deceptively, Africa is faring well compared to Oceania/Australia with a total population of over 36 million people. Considering the size of the population in each of these two regions, the reality emerges that the African continent has the largest population whose voice(s) is/are not (re)presented in the digital space. Even with this question of (re)presentation in the digital space aside, in the traditional analog spaces there already exists an asymmetry in the power to (re)present, with roots harking back to colonization and has even been heightened in and by the contemporary processes of globalization. It is expected that this asymmetry will achieve a new dimension in the context of the fast evolving information and communication technologies that have widened socio-cultural spaces. Inevitably, as such emerging spaces come into being, contestations on representation are either escalated from the offline spaces or are given new, albeit subtler dimensions. Other than such escalations and emergent forms of representation of others in this evolving spaces, new forms of subalternity brought into being.

Quite often, images filtering through both the online and offline media have continued to portray the continent and its peoples in unfavourable terms, sterilizing it of the human narratives. In 'How to Write About Africa,' Binyavanga Wainaina wryly documents the images of Africa and its societies as would characterize the text as *the* legitimate representation of Africa, in which the humanizing threads are silenced:

> Taboo subjects: ordinary domestic scenes, love between Africans (unless a death is involved), references to African writers or intellectuals, mention of school-going children who are not suffering from yaws or Ebola fever or female genital mutilation. (Wainaina 92)
>
> Broad brushstrokes throughout are good. Avoid having the African characters laugh, or struggle to educate their kids, or just make do in mundane circumstances. Have them illuminate something about Europe or America in Africa. African characters should be colourful, exotic, larger than life—but empty inside, with no dialogue, no conflicts or resolutions in their stories, no depth or quirks to confuse the cause. (Wainaina 94)

In the textual world conjured up by an 'African writer' alluded to by Wainaina, Africans are not endowed with the capacity to imagine their own being in the flux of their own socio-cultural universe. The text imagined by Wainaina purports to translate the Other world in terms legitimated by the translator's position with the consequence that the humans in that world assume a form amenable to the (un)declared interests of the translator.

The consequence of this silencing of the lived experience in Africa parallels the sociocultural erasure not dissimilar to colonial representation on which, as often asserted, the colonial subjugation was founded. For example, in *Orientalism*, a constant reference text on the ulterior representation of Other, Edward Said has fleshed out the processes by which the colonial/imperial textuality subtly embroiled the media spaces in the colonial complicity (see also Said 1980). As Wainaina sums it up, the images of African societies in the contemporary Western media spaces are to portray the putative benevolence of the hegemonic Western society, whereas the undeclared intention, as he tacitly implies, is to justify procedures of ('philanthropic') interventions (Wainaina 95). On the other hand, the colonial portrayals of Africa – as it is now commonly argued - in the context of colonial textuality, served to justify colonial occupation and exploitation in the name of the 'civilizing mission.' Chinua Achebe has convincingly argued that Africans were represented as inchoate, primordial, even subhuman. The subject of his analysis is Joseph Conrad's *Heart of Darkness*, a text with declared anticolonial intentions but which come off as complicit in denigrating the subjects of colonialism in its representation of Africans as cultureless physical forms (Achebe 1975, 1786; NooriBerzenji and Abdi 710).

The Concept Of Hypertextuality

The present task confronts the possibility of practice and transfer of Afro-literary art to the digital space. It is undergirded by the premise that the internet has brought with it an alternative online, if not an extension of, reality for cultural articulation, the absence of which constitutes a parallel to the historical muting of the discursive cultural voices of the global margins. In reflecting on that possibility, it observes that cyber-representation is grounded on a language and technologies different from the offline orality and/or 'writtenness' of the African literary art. Embracing the language and the technologies of the cyberspace, the basic argument is that hypertext, the language of internet, and hypermedia, the digital space afforded by the hypertext, provide a now front for representations of self and Others.

As deployed here, hypertextuality suggests not so much the system that over-determines and/or collaborates with the literary text to render a specific significance, as to the possibility of Afro-literary arts in the digital space bequeathing what David Farkas terms 'information scent' that inter-navigates them by means of hypertext and hypermedia (Farkas 3). As implied in the foregoing, the conception of hypertextuality draws from that of textuality 'as the meaning structure(s) of the text' (Silverman 55), a meaning grid within which the significance of a literary text is knitted (Said 675). Whereas textuality suggests how a text is read and, concurrently, how it renders itself to be so read, the way the constituent textual elements are interlinked and inter-related in the lineal act of reading, hypertextuality refers to the discursive cyber-existence of a text. It is the manner in which the web texts are discursively 'noded' by means of hypertext and hypermedia (Farkas 2), as to render themselves to digital (re)mobilization by the criteria of their forms, content filiations, internet user's own online activity, interests, and to some extent even their location. As Ernst Grabovszki puts it, as a text is inserted into the digital sphere, it at once digitally transforms into a network, of itself and of other texts, each with a multiplicity of authorship (5). With reference to Afro-literary art, it implies the filial/filiative relations of the art in the digital space, the authorial cyber-dispersal (in the Foucauldian sense), the cyber-scattering and cyber-recuperation of the text.

Hypertextuality and Voice

As pointed out above, the internet penetration in the continent of Africa puts it at a disadvantage in the cultural presence in the digital space. The direct result of this is the marginality of the Afro-voice in this digital frontier and the possible (re)presentation by Others. Ananda Mitra and

Eric Watts have pointed out that the internet is a discursive phenomenon in which interest groups, and by extension, diverse cultures, voice themselves in ways different from, and even transcending, their offline reality (481). Without access to the internet and the proficiency in its usage, the cyberspace Afro-voice mirrors the marginality of the same in the 'international' analog spaces of self-(re)presentation.

At the same time as the internet statistics noted above point at the minority of continental Africa in the internet, they also indicate an optimistic trend in the uptake of the internet technology. Internet World Stats shows that between 2000 and 2013, there was a 5219.6% growth of internet penetration in Africa, the most phenomenal rate compared to other continents. However, it is worth noting that this statistics are continental and do not capture the nationalities of internet users in each continent: there are, for example, Canadian nationals resident in Africa, citizens from African countries resident in other continents, who access internet in continents other than their own.

This has two implications: the internet penetration in Africa could either be worse or better than is represented by Internet World Stats. This raises again the question of diaspora and its relation to Africa. As pertains Mitra and Watts's idea of voice in the internet discourse, the African diaspora, especially in the Euro-American metropolis, is arguably instrumental in engendering the Afro-voice in the digital space inasmuch as they carry with them the African experience and reside in the technology saturated countries. These diasporic experiences in turn beget the next question: do the voices of the African diaspora constitute the authentic voices of the multitudes of *in situ* Africans? Mitra reflects on this question of legitimacy of (re)presentation and makes an imperative call that the validity of voice in the cyberspace ought to be regarded vis-á-vis the speaker's location, as locations as such are fraught with ideological significances (Trust, Authenticity, and Discursive Power in the Cyberspace 28). Critical here is the question of the hypertextual voices of the African populations which do not access the internet. How do their stories form part of the digital world in a way that their legitimacy is maintained? By what process is their digital modes of self-(re)presentation in the literary art be possible? In an attempt to answer these questions, translation is offered here as a process for the cyber-voicing of the Afro-literary art.

Since the language and the nature of the medium that constitute the cyberspace is different from the language and the nature of the offline spaces, the voices in the latter spaces can only be inserted in this digital space through the process of translation. As a necessary point of departure, the notion that the internet is both a medium and a space coterminous with the offline reality and at a continuum with it has to be embraced.

In order to prefigure my subsequent argument concerning analog-digital translation, it is crucial to restate a point about the technological ontology of hypertextuality. Hypertextuality can only be achieved by means of hypertext and hypermedia, which are constituted of electronic codes. Mistra reminds us that '[b]eing digital recodes the analog real into intangible electronic signals reducing the entire analog experience to a combination of "on" and "off" switch positions designated by a "1" or "0" respectively' (Mitra, Cybernetic Space: Bringing the Virtual and the Real Together 3). The digital space is thus a function of electronic codes: 'a set of computer programs, codes, and machine languages distributed on computers' (Mitra, Cybernetic Space: Bringing the Virtual and the Real Together 3). This is so much as to say that the cyberspace exists courtesy of this sort of *language* into which the analog world is necessarily translated as *sine qua non* of the realization of the virtual world. To conjure up the digital world, the electronic codes act in conjunction with computer programs to, first, bring into being the medium (digital space); secondly, the electronic codes are the means by which the forms within this medium are realized. Into this electronic *code* (in linguistic sense) is the verbal, visual and written analog sign transferred. From this, one may then pose: doesn't this transfer implicate the process of translation? Isn't an internet code developer a translator of some sort engaging in the translation of analog reality?

In the following premises, an affirmative answer to the question will be worked out and afterwards, its implication will be deliberated on.

Offline-Online Transfers As Translation

The concept of translation indisputably bears a heavy inflection of the term's usage in the linguistic understanding of transfer of meaning across linguistic boundaries. This understanding has had a cross-disciplinary significance, with cultural studies particularly finding an invaluable use for it (Orsini and Srivastava 324-5). The translational needs for the intercultural communication take cognisance of the linguistic concept but transcend it for the purpose of understanding the processes involved in intercultural relations. In the words of Mary Louise Pratt, translation becomes a 'metaphor for analyzing intercultural interaction and transaction' (25).

First, though, preliminary questions: When does transfer of 'meaning' or 'sense,' especially one which is a socio-cultural property, from one media platform to another pass as a translational activity? What does the transfer involve in terms of expressive forms employed for the purposes of such transfer? Can one at all refer to transfer of analog realities into

Language and Translation

the cyberspace as translation? To demonstrate the translational nature of digital-analog transfers, one can turn to the practices in the transfer of musical sounds across various media spaces.

Musical sounds can be represented by use of either of two systems of notation, staff notation and Sol-Fah notation. Staff notations are the signs operating in the staff as a representational space, whereas Sol-fa notations are quasi-linguistic forms involving punctuation marks and standard quasi-syllabic units, the sol-fa. The two notation systems work independently of one another, though the notation in one can be transferred appropriately to the other. The opening melodic phrase (*sound content*; 'meaning' or 'sense') of the Kenya National Anthem is represented with staff notation (*forms*) as follows:

(Source: (*Ring Round the World: National Anthem Sheet Music*)

The same sound content above can be represented with Sol-fa notation thus:

Lah = A (Doh = C)
Time signature = $\frac{44}{44}$

r^I r^I :. r^I. d^I : s   l: 1   _: r^I r^I : 1 . 1 d^I : d^I

(Source: (*Ring Round the World: National Anthem Sheet Music*)

From the above, it is apparent that translation is necessarily defined in terms of transfer of content from one kind of notation (*format*) to another. As attested to by the notations above, musical form basically serve to represent an aural stimulus as accurately as possible – the anthem, for example, will always remain unchanged but the notation (the *form*) may change. In other words, the authenticity of the national anthem is assured despite the variety of the codes which are used to represent it. The translation of the melody from sol-fa notation (quasi-linguistic medium) to staff medium involves a violation of form for the purpose of transferring a meaning or sense.

One can thus add that in translating, sense or meaning is transferred from one form or medium (as a configuration of forms) to another: for example, from one language to another, from one culture to another, from one media space to another. We can begin here then to regard the process of culturally voicing oneself in the digital world from the perspective of translation. Analog data are themselves translated into electronic codes.

In our case, the literary data – the linguistic signs (verbal and written), which constitute the text(s), are necessarily dispensed with in the process of digital-analog translation.

The emergence of the digital space adds a new dimension to the idea of translation. But as often asserted, the cyberspace mirrors the reality outside of it and as such, retain a semblance of it. The digital space presents semblances of the analog, but only as façades of the quintessential digital into which the analogs necessarily have to be translated by means of hypertextual and hypermedial reduction. In the light of Afro-literary art, the literary text on the internet, as seen on the screen of an online computer becomes a manifestation of a hypertextual Afro-story inserted into the digital space by the electronic code writer, *as translator*.

One undeniable purpose of the digital space is the ideological (re)presentation of offline realities. As pointed out, the image of Africa and Africans in the Western media spaces, as Binyavanga Wainaina imagines, largely disconnects from the realities in the various corners of Africa. However, this need not be the case in every instance since the digital world may as well be unique from the analog sphere or may afford possibilities that are uncharacteristic of the analog world. Despite this, however, in circumstances where attempt is made to extend the analog voices into the digital sphere, this is when translation is implicated as the process by which that offline reality is voiced in the digital space. After all, for any cultural group intending to utter themselves in this digital sphere, what overrides all else is the authenticity of that cultural utterance, rather than – as Mitra puts it – the 'bits and bytes feverishly working together to create images, texts, and sounds' (re)presentative of the culture in question (Mitra, Cybernetic Space: Bringing the Virtual and the Real Together 3). Mitra aptly describes the behind-the-scene workings of the electronic language functioning under the tyranny of the imperative to authentically (con)figure the hitherto analog cultural self.

Conclusion

The foregoing enables us to observe a number of issues, all of which are intertwined. The Africa continent trails other continents in terms of access and, therefore, use of the internet. The implication of this is that there are questions regarding their (re)presentation in the digital space, one of which is that the peoples of Africa whose voices are not heard in it would have to contend with digital subalternity, or the consequence of being (mis/re)presented in terms other than their own, as paralleled by the reality outside of this digital space. As a means to enabling them engender their authentic voice in the digital world, translation was offered here as process by which their analog cultural reality can be voiced in that cyberspace.

References

Achebe, Chinua. "An Image of Africa: Racism in Conrad's Heart of Darkness." University of Massachusetts, February 1975. 1783-1794. Web. 25 November 2013. <http://wayanswardhani.lecture.ub.ac.id/files/2013/05/Achebe-1.pdf>.—. *Things Fall Apart*. Nairobi: East African Educational Publishers, 1966. print.

Bhabha, Homi. "Of Mimicry and Man: The Ambivalence of Colonial Discourse." *Discipleship: A Special Issue on Psychoanalysis* 28.Spring (1984): 125-133. Document. 28 November 2013. < http://www.jstor.org/stable/778467>.

Cartmell, Deborah and Imelda Whelehan, *Adaptations: From Text to Screen, Srceen to Text*. London: Routledge, 1999.

Farkas, David K. "Hypertext and Hypermedia." *Berkshire Encyclopedia of Human-Computer Interaction* (2004): 332-336. Document. 5 October 2014. <http://faculty.washington.edu/farkas/dfpubs/Farkas-Hypertext%20And%20Hypermedia.pdf>.

Frantz, Fanon. *The Wretched of the Earth*. Trans. Richard Philcox. 1st. New York: Grove Press, 2004.

Grabovszki, Ernst. "The Impact of Globalization and the New Media on the Notion of World Literature." *CLCWeb: Comparative Literature and Culture* 1.3 (1999): 2-8. Document.

Internet World Stats. *Internet Users in the World*. Ed. Enrique de Argaez. 18 September 2014. Miniwatts Marketing Group . Electronic. 10 October 2014. <http://www.internetworldstats.com/stats.htm>.

Iser, Wolfgang. *The Act of Reading: A Theory of Aesthetic Response*. London: Routledge & Keagan Paul, 1978. Print.

Macmillan Dictionary. *Discourse*. 2013. Web. 20 November 2013. <http://www.macmillandictionary.com/dictionary/british/discourse>.

Maritim, Eric C. *The Female Character in Kawabata Yasunari: Sources, Form and Implicatures*. Saarbrucken: LAP LAMBERT, 2012. Print.

Mitra, Ananda and Eric Watts. "Theorizing Cyberspace: The Idea of Voice Applied to the Internet Discourse." *New Media Society* 4 (2002): 479-498. Document.

Mitra, Ananda. "Cybernetic Space: Bringing the Virtual and the Real Together." *Journal of Interactive Advertising* 3.2 (2003): 1-9. Electronic. 11 October 2014. <http://jiad.org/downloadc7e3.pdf?p=31>.—. "Trust, Authenticity, and Discursive Power in the Cyberspace." *Communications of the ACM* 45.3 (2002): 27-29. Document. <https://www.student.cs.uwaterloo.ca/~cs492/10public_html/.../trust.pdf>.

NooriBerzenji, Latef S. and Marwan Abdi. "The Image of the Africans in Heart of Darkness and Things Fall Apart." *Interdisciplinary Journal of Contemporary Research in Business* 5.4 (2013): 710-726. Web. 29 November 2013. <ijcrb.webs.com>.

Orsini, Francesca and Neelam Srivastava. "Translation and the Postcolonial." *Interventions: International Journal of Postcolonial Studies* 15.3 (2013): 323-331. Web. 9 11 2013.

Osuji, Chuks. *The Myth of Kola Nut*. 10 February 2013. Web. 4 December 2013. <file:///C:/Users/Martin/Desktop/The%20myth%20behind%20kola%20nut%20_%20Daily%20Independent%20Newspapers.htm>.

—. *The Myth of Kola Nut 2*. 3 March 2013. <http://dailyindependentnig.com/2013/03/the-myth-behind-kola-nut-2/>.

Pratt, Mary Louise. "The Traffic in Meaning: Translation, Contagion, Infiltration." *Proffesion* (2002): 25-36. Web. 23 10 2013. <http://www.jstor.org/stable/25595727>.

Ring Round the World: National Anthem Sheet Music. n.d. Web. 20 09 2013.

Said, Edward. "Islam Through Western Eyes." *The Nation* 26 April 1980. Web. <http://www.thenation.com/article/islam-through-western-eyes>.

—. *Orientalism*. London: Penguin, 1977. <www.odsg.org/Said_Edward(1977)_Orientalism.pdf□>.

—. "The Problem of Textuality: Two Exemplary Positions." *Critical Inquiry* 4.4 (1978): 673-714. Document.

Sanders, Julie. *Adaptation and Appropriation*. Oxford: Routlegde, 2006. Print.

Schmidt-Jones, Catherine. *Transposition: Changing Keys*. n.d. Web. 15 10 2013. <http://cnx.org/content/m10668/latest/>.

Silverman, Hugh J. "What is Textuality?" *Phenomenology + Pedagogy* 4.2 (1986): 54-61. Document.

Taylor, Charles. *Modern Social Imaginaries*. Durham, NC: Duke University Press, 2004. Web. 20 November 2013. <http://books.google.co.tz/books?id=5vFjlflzod8C&printsec=frontcover&source=gbs_ge_summary_r&cad=0#v=onepage&q&f=false>.

UNESCO. *Cultural Diversity*. n.d. 28 10 2013. <http://www.unesco.org/new/en/social-and-human-sciences/themes/international-migration/glossary/cultural-diversity/>.

Wainaina, Binyavanga. "How to Write About Africa." *Granta: The Magazine of New Writing* 92 (2005). Web. 25 November 2013.

Chapter Three

African Images in Kenya Film as a Response to Colonial "Misrepresentations"

Rachael Diang'a and Oluoch Obura

Introduction

For many African filmmakers, cinematic expression is closely linked to decolonization, a theme that has largely dominated the post-independent creative works in the continent[1]. In most African countries, filmmaking gained roots after independence. Consequently, African filmmakers have used film to bring out the impact of Western ideologies on Africans.[2] The African has been portrayed as a debased individual in various works of literature. This portrayal is part of the false historical and cultural ideology formed about the African, which is best disseminated by cinema—and its by-product, television (Bakupa 2004). According to Michael Parker and Rodger Starkey, this image "...can be seen in much of the television representation of Africa by the Western media, which portrays Africa in perpetual crisis and continues to fix the indigenous peoples as passive, infectiously smiling or suffering backdrops for white politicians and aid workers" (1995, 6). Recently, subversion of the image of the African in cinema has emerged as an area of interest to many scholars[3]. Formally or informally, several Kenyan filmmakers have shown specific concern about the image of the African as portrayed in the western film, admitting that re-presenting the African is one of their major roles[4]. A case in point is Anne Mungai, a Kenyan filmmaker who says that in general, this is one of the several concerns of an African filmmaker[5].

Mungai's position is shared by Wanjiru Kinyanjui, another Kenyan filmmaker, who believes it is her duty to re-present the African through film. She says:

in every film I do, I try to correct the negative image we have of ourselves by trying to portray Africans, from the human side. Of course human beings err, and are never perfect, but there are also positive sides to us, which never surface in films made by outsiders. These I try to include in my films. And if I portray a character as basically negative, it is because we also have such characters, which (sic) exist everywhere. It is a quest to question, to probe, to rediscover qualities using cinema as a tool[6].

From these filmmakers' sentiments, this study postulates that among other preoccupations of Kenyan filmmakers, responding to the portrayal of the African in Western film is pivotal. This is however a claim of responsibility whose validity needs to be established. Therefore, this study is an endeavour to ascertain whether these claims are evident in two Kenyan films: Sao Gamba's *Kolormask* (1986) and Wanjiru Kinyanjui's *The Battle of the Sacred Tree* (1994).In so doing, the study draws from the "negative" portrayal of the Africans in two Western films, Harry Cook's *The Kitchen Toto* and Sydney Pollack's *Out of Africa*, as a backdrop of analysis for the two Kenyan films.

The second part of the problem that this study investigates rests on the nature of the existing studies on Kenyan film. In reviewing these works, the research found that very few studies paid attention to the image and re-presentation of the African in the Kenyan film. These studies (Beatrice Mukora, 2003 and Beti Elerson 2000) based their focus on the African woman. However, one gets the impression that the African woman is metonymically viewed as a representative of the African fraternity. These studies are quite atomic in their approach and fail to give an overall picture or portrayal of the African in the Kenyan film. The current study therefore attempts a more holistic investigation of the (re-)presentation of the African, whether male or female, child or adult. In following these two threads, the study identifies the images assigned to the African in the sampled Western films then interrogates the impact of these images on the re-presentation of the African in the selected Kenyan films.

Very little study has been conducted on the film industry in Kenya. As such, no research has focused on re-presentation of the African through film. This study aims to locate the different images of the African along the history of filmmaking in Kenya. The need to re-present the image of the African has emerged to be of great concern in post-independent African literature.[7] Maureen Eke, Kenneth Harrow and Emmanuel Yewah see the need to support issues of representation and image of the African in African literature and cinema (1975:7). It is this recreation of self-image that Chinua Achebe refers to as "re-creating the past in the present" (2000:79). This study therefore emerges as one of the contributions towards the corpus of this concern.

The study is positioned within postcoloniality, exploring such precepts as the colonising cultures' distortion of the experience and realities of the colonised people, inscribing inferiority of the latter in the cultural artefacts of the former. Thus the discussion in this study majorly reflects on the discourses surrounding key concepts in this theoretical standpoint such as the "centre" and its "margins" or the "self" and the "other" (John Lye 1997). The study is keen to examine the impact of these classifications on the cultural products of the former colonies.

The Film Industry in Kenya

The development of a film industry is usually closely related to quantity and consequently quality of feature film production in a country or region. Some of the earliest attempts at feature filmmaking in Kenya were seen in the early sixties just after television was introduced in the country in 1962. *Mrembo* and *Mlevi* are among the films made in this period. However there are no clear records indicating their exact year of production. However, Simiyu's (2010) documentary film, *History of Film in Kenyan: 1909 - 2009* associates the two films with Kuljit Pal, and Ragbil Pal, two Kenyan brothers of Asian descent. These films dealt with the day-to-day social issues such as the effects of alcoholism. From that time, the genre received scant attention until the production of *Kolormask* in 1986. The production of *Kolormask* was a result of the activities of the now defunct Kenya Film Corporation, which collapsed after the film was released. KFC, the first of its kind in sub-Saharan Africa, was formed in 1967 by the Kenyan government and was in charge of all film activities in the country including importation and distribution. It was also in charge of film production but only managed to produce the first Kenyan feature film, *Kolormask*, directed by the late Sao Gamba.

While Kenya boasts good filming locations and few but capable crew and cast members, it wasn't until the 1990s that consistent film production was witnessed in the country. It is in this decade that films like *Saikati I* and *Saikati II* (1992), *Saikati the Enkabaani* (1997), *Metamo* (1997), *The Battle of the Sacred Tree* (1994), *Sabina's Encounter* (1998), and *The Married Bachelor* (1997), among others, were released. Kenya had slowly and steadily increased the rate of film production by the turn of the millennium. Filmmaking had risen to yet another level with individual film-houses exhibiting their capacity to produce more than three films within a year.

Particular thematic inclinations can be observed in Kenya films. Apart from the Pals' early films, which highlighted social issues such as the impact of alcoholism, cultural reaffirmation in *Kolormask* was meant to set the pace for later films. *Kolormask* holds a very significant position in the history of filmmaking in Kenya. It was made using state funds and it revolves around the cultural differences between John, an England trained Kenyan doctor and his British housewife, Eliza. The film juxtaposes the two to highlight the subversive change of power that many African colonies assumed soon after independence. With reference to this family, power shifts from the coloniser to the colonised. According to Mukora (2003,227), "indigenous filmmaking in Kenya began as a counter-colonial discourse similar to that found in the work of such novelists as Meja Mwangi, Grace Ogot, and Ngugi wa Thiong'o." *Kolormask* aimed at contributing to this debate.

The discussions preceding the production of *Kolormask* reflected some of the manifestos, declarations and resolutions which had been made concerning African cinema. From the early 1970s, African filmmakers and other prominent cineastes deliberated on the possible use of 'third world cinema' as a popular tool of re-making history. They saw cinema as a means of seeking cultural liberation and progress. For example, they observed that African cinema needed a commitment for it to assert the cultural identity of the Africans. They also recommended that African governments support national film industries in terms of policies, financial assistance and distribution of films. Several Governments were also to establish national film corporations to centralize all matters pertaining to cinema in these countries. In Kenya, most of these propositions were realized when the state funded the production of *Kolormask* through the then active Kenya Film Corporation. *Kolormask*'s theme is in line with the pan-African thoughts that informed most creative works in the post-independent African countries at that time.

Portrayal of the African in the Western Films

This study delves into the supposedly negative images by which Africans are associated in two films, namely, Sydney Pollack's *Out of Africa* (1987) and Harry Hook's *The Kitchen Toto* (1985). *Out of Africa*, a Hollywood production from Universal Pictures, is set in the 1914 colonial Kenya, and is based on Isak Dinesen's 1934 memoir of her life there.

Tarzan series, directed by Edgar Rice Burroughs, had some of the earliest Hollywood presentations of Africa through film. Although he never set foot on African soil Burroughs created fictional images of Africa as well as his legendary character, Tarzan, who was to fascinate generations of Americans and audiences everywhere. Due to the popularity of Burroughs' romance stories, they inspired a series of Hollywood films. With such films, "Hollywood Commercial Cinema exploited the popular misconceptions already embedded in the African romance-adventure stories of the 19th century writers" (Ukadike 1994, 40). In an attempt to appeal to cinema audiences' taste for exoticism at the expense of exploiting the Africans, racist European texts have continued to be adapted for the Hollywood screen. This later led to the production of films such as *King Solomon's Mines* (1937), *Ghost and The Darkness* (1996), *Hatari* (1962) and *Out of Africa* (1987), among others.

The Kitchen Toto (1985) is a British production relating some of the political experiences in 1950s Kenya, a time when Mau Mau resistance reached its peak. The two films do not only share the fact that they are both based on reality but also two issues this study deems important. First, they are both exoteric presentations of Kenya through the eyes of Western directors. Second, the films present post-independence tales of the colonial experience in Kenya.

By analysing the African as depicted in these two Western films, the study is, however, aware that it is not only the Africans whose image has been portrayed negatively in film. It is common to find negative images of the third world in colonial literature and (their adaptation into) film. These works have, in one way or another, presented the colonised as lesser beings. Michael Harris says,

The continuing appeal of fictional portrayals of the colonies is perhaps even more evident in film. Adaptations of *Kim, King Solomon's Mines, Mister Johnson, A Passage to India, The Raj Quartet, Heat and Dust, The Far Pavilions*, Elspeth Huxley's *The Flame Trees of Thika* and Isak Dinesen's *Out of Africa* have been made...for cinema and television. Thus, Western audiences receive a view of the so-called Third World that is largely unchanged from that put forward by the British writers during the colonial era. (Harris 1994, 26)

Most colonial films were based on Charles Darwin's theory of evolution, which justified the popular "supremacy" of the coloniser in the face of the colonised (Darwin 1859). The popularity of this colonial mentality was enhanced largely by colonial works of fiction, which included film. In *Orientalism*, Edward Saïd argues that these portrayals were enhanced by the development of cinematography. With the invention of "television, the film and all the media's resources" we came to witness "a reinforcement of the stereotypes by which the orient (and all 'others') are viewed" (1978, 26). To Robert Stam and Louise Spence, these "others" include "the long parade [in films] of lazy Mexicans, shifty Arabs, savage Africans and exotic Asiatics" (in Ukadike 1994, 36).[8] To the African, the most significant factor that this kind of creative work disseminates is "perhaps the negative image accorded to the African character. It is as if everything that is said about the African is intended to demean" (Chemjor1998, 30). Postcolonialist theory argues that colonial contact is, to a large extent, the genesis of such demeaning portrayals. At the time when abolition of slave trade and slavery heightened in the nineteenth century, colonisation of Africa and racism were, however, on the rise. Portraying the colonial subjects negatively in film was, therefore, one of the means by which colonial empires in Africa sustained pre-eminence.

It should, however, be noted that Africans have not just been presented negatively throughout the history of Western cinema. In as much as such Western films have been blamed for distorting the image of Africans, some of these films have worked towards the need for the emancipation of the African from the prejudiced depiction. *The Black Oblivion* (2003) gives a much improved image of the African.

In Sydney Pollack's *Out of Africa*, Karen leaves her Danish homeland to marry a British man, Baron Bror Blixen Finecke in the Kenya of 1914. Although Karen and Bror have planned to engage in dairy farming in Kenya, they end up in coffee farming. This makes her relate closely with the local communities. It is from this relationship that Pollack's depiction of the Africans is clearly observed. Through the relationship between the local population and the colonisers or settlers, the viewer observes certain trends in Pollack's characterization.

Pollack's *Out of Africa* pieces together the episodes in Isak Dinesen's memoir into a continuous narrative. To remain artistically viable, the film—scripted by Kurt Luedtke—selectively highlights scenes that together foreground the settler/coloniser's life in colonial Kenya. The film, however, relegates the African to the background. The individual attention that Dinesen pays to the Africans in the novel is thus subverted in the film. Even though Dinesen's targeted audience is by all indications Western, her vivid description of the "natives," the farm and Africa in general makes her work more focused on Africa (Dinesen 1937). In the film, this focus shifts to the Western characters. The film's plot centres on Karen's love life and farming. For instance, Karen's marriage to Bror and her love affair with the British adventurer and big game hunter, Denys Finch-Hatton, receive more attention in the film than in the novel. This exemplifies Pollack's point of departure from Dinesen's novel. Pollack's change of focus can, therefore, be viewed as one of the opportunities available for a filmmaker who adapts another work of art into film. This selectivity is usually guided by a filmmaker's preference, which is in turn determined by the interests of his/her targeted audience, evidently Western.

There is a very close relationship between the African characters and animals in the film, *Out of Africa*. This is evident in the fascination the squatter children get when the miniature bird perched on Karen Blixen's clock cuckoos at the top of every hour. These children are portrayed to have developed a special liking for the "bird." This friendship, however, is not shared with Karen. While the throng of children crowd her doorway, she seems so engrossed in her work that she is not even aware of their presence by her door. When the children abruptly take off in excitement,

Karen notices them for the first time. The impression this scene creates is that the children find it much easier to identify with the animal, even if it is an artificial imitation, than with Karen. The children visit Karen's house to see the bird thus viewing Karen's interest in talking to them as an intrusion.

The manner in which the children take off can be compared to the confused movements of zebras running from the car in which Karen and Denys drive. Another similarity is implied by the posture of the buffaloes and that of Africans, which are both followed by abrupt take-off, at the appearance of the settler/coloniser. Group shots are characteristic of scenes with Africans, and animals. Such shots include Africans queuing up for treatment, working in the coffee plantation, mesmerised by Denys' aircraft and running in amazement just like the wild game viewed from the plane on Karen's way to Mombasa. Similarity of the two can create the illusion that both share demeanour and way of life.

Pollack creates an illusory perception of the African as a close variant of the monkey. The Kikuyu children's conversation and the squeaking of monkeys outside Karen's house are fused in one scene and made to sound similar. The children's conversations may seem to be originating from the monkeys playing among them and vice versa. Gianeti Battetini (1996:111) believes that "the essence of the cinema is basically visual and every sonic intervention ought to limit itself to a *justified and necessary act of expressive integration*" (emphasis added). This requires that only *justified* and *necessary* sound components are implicitly foregrounded such that they emphasise meaning.

For an exoteric viewer (Pollack's targeted audience), it is not easy to see the difference between the two languages—monkey and native—that co-exist in this scene. The film presents them as just some noises from the "other". For a keener viewer, and one who understands Kikuyu, the revelation of the implied conversation between the monkeys and the natives can be disturbing.

For colonial cinema, portraying the African in such a romanticised and limiting manner would serve the colonialist inscriber's emotional, psychological and social interests by proving the latter's superiority. The British Empire's superiority played a major role in the survival of the colonial regime. However, viewing such portrayals in *Out of Africa* today may have varying allegorical implications, depending on the viewer and his/her background.

On viewing the film, one notices a pattern that facilitates the notion that Africans are unintelligent. Fanon wrote that a close variation of the animal simile in the depiction of Africans in colonial fiction is the child (see Fanon 1967), meaning that Africans are made to reason like small children, who without the help of the adult—represented by the colonier/settler—cannot make rational decisions. In *Out of Africa*, the "squatters" are depicted as children who cannot take care of themselves in the absence of Karen. When Karen finally leaves for Denmark after having become bankrupt, she asks Farah, her trusted servant, to "make them believe that I will not always be there to speak for them." Viewing the Africans as not capable of speaking for themselves has far-reaching effects as the film unfolds. The Africans come to believe that they really are incapacitated. This is why when Karen is about to leave for Denmark, Farah still hopes to follow her and find her on the way. Farah finds it difficult to live without Karen, whom he has served for a long time.

Karen implies her ownership of the natives and her parental role to them. She says she always knew *her* squatters' children. She justifies her possession of the squatters at the New Year ball when she says to Denys:

Karen:	...you don't think they (the Kikuyu) should learn to read?
Denys:	I think you'd better ask them.
Karen:	Did your mother ask you when you were a young child?
Denys	...Did you want to change them?
Karen:	...I want *my* Kikuyu to learn to read.

When Denys cautions her about her tendency to possess the Africans, she strongly puts it that "I pay the price for everything I own." To her enlightening the Kikuyu by teaching them to read is the self-imposed cost of being their guardian. Likening the African to children uplifts Karen's position to that of an adult, a thinker, source of livelihood, of health and ultimately source of life. She believes that she should guide the Kikuyu just the way Denys' mother supposedly did to Denys when he was a child. For instance, Karen knows that she is not a medical practitioner but she goes ahead and administers medication to the squatters. They visit her in larger numbers day by day. They get better although Karen admits that she does not know how.

Vaughan says that in Hollywood epics' depiction of the African, "the African people play either scenery props (picturesque crowds with spears) or curiously unintelligent menials" (quoted in Ukadike1994: 41). The latter part of his description explains the roles assigned to the Africans in *Out of Africa*. The semi-skilled labourers that work on Karen's coffee farm provide the scenes with a complete picture of Karen's efforts to keep busy the otherwise lazy natives. In most cases, they appear in groups, representing the orderliness the settler/colonialist has imparted on them. A similar scenario is observed when the natives queue for medication at Karen's house.

Pollack, in this film, tends to focus more on the jungle, the environment, more than the Africans who populate it, rekindling the significance of his target audience. Linked to this is the plurality with which the Africans are addressed. Words like "the natives," "the Kikuyu" and "the Maasai" indicate that none of these are part of her intended audience. They are, therefore, exempted from the audience even though they feature as vital plot enhancers, creating suspense and excitement in the story (Ukadike 1994, 37).

As opposed to the Hollywood explorative films, for the British, justification for occupying Africa was a more important concern than cinematic exploitation of exotic décor. This explains why most British colonial films reflected the ideological currents that were propelled by the British imperial government. *The Post Office Savings Bank* and *The Tax* are some of the 1930s colonial films made in East Africa that attest to the above statement. The films presented Africa and its native peoples as a locus for the European civilising mission.

After the 1884 sscramble for Africa meeting in Berlin, the European countries took it upon themselves to "civilise" Africans. The pioneers, who first introduced cinema in Africa, argued the same (Diawara 1992, 1). Realising that commercial films, like those of Charlie Chaplin, could show the colonies the negative side of the European and North American life, these pioneers lead by Major L. A. Notcutt, decided that:

With backward peoples unable to distinguish between truth and falsehood, it is surely in our wisdom, if not our obvious duty, to prevent as far as possible the dissemination of wrong ideas. Should we stand by and see a distorted presentation of the white race's life accepted by millions of Africans when we have it in our power to show them the truth? (in Diawara 1992, 1 and Ngayane 1998/1999, 12)

The British spearheaded this move by creating the Bantu Educational Cinema Experiment (BECE).[9]

By 1939, the British set up Colonial Film Units (CFU), with branches in East, Central and West Africa. The CFUs distributed films, which aimed at spreading propaganda, which would help enlist Africans to take part in World War II. This required that films from Europe and North America be re-edited to suit this goal. There was, however, a concealed motive in re-editing films from the West for the African audience. Jean Rouch says, "if the immediate goal of the Colonial Film Unit was to make war propaganda, its organiser, W. Sellers, in fact, had in mind a long-range project – establishing a systematic way to utilise film with an African audience" (Rouch in Diawara 1992, 3). After the war, the CFU's role changed from distribution to production. The films produced aimed at convincing Africans to adopt Western etiquette.

These activities officially justified colonial misrepresentation of Africans in film. Coalitions such as the National Association for the Advancement of Coloured People (NAACP) in America have worked towards the positive portrayal of Africans and the African Diaspora. Many voices for change in Africa have also expressed similar sentiments since independence.[10] In spite of such efforts, portrayal of the African has continued to be negative in films made long after political independence of the African states. Ukadike says "partial or falsified images of Africa have not ceased and... the desire to make a profit continues to be the basic motivation for this endless exploitation" (1994, 58). The motivation may have changed from spreading colonial ideology to profit making but the impact has been the same—cultural displacement of the African. An example of these films is Harry Hook's *The Kitchen Toto*.

The Kitchen Toto tells the story of two families: one of an African pastor, Kariuki and the other of a colonial policeman, John Graham. Both families become victims of the terrorising Mau Mau fighters. Two distinct groups emerge in the film: the British colonisers and the African squatters. Mwangi, the first son of pastor Kariuki, loses his father in a furious Mau Mau attack on his family after Kariuki refuses to yield to the demands of the Mau Mau fighters. Mwangi, pushed by circumstances, gets employed as Graham's kitchen toto. It is during his stay at Graham's that the viewer gets to understand Mwangi better.

Unlike Pollack, Hook creates Mwangi's background in a stable family. As the film begins, we see a still photograph portrait of Mwangi's family. This enables the viewer to understand Mwangi in relation to his relatives. Yet, the fact that the whole of Mwangi's family is introduced does not improve the viewer's perception of the African character in any way. Mwangi's family is used to draw the viewer's attention to the cruelty of the Mau Mau fighters. It grieves the audience to see the happy family being torn apart by the ruthless gang led by Kamau. Hook seems to have taken a position different from most colonial filmmakers by anchoring the African in a family. Nevertheless, the colonial master and not Mwangi's loved ones determines the latter's traits. This comes out in the manner in which Graham treats Mwangi when Mrs Graham is accidentally shot dead by her son, Edward. Despite the help Mwangi offers Graham's family by alerting them to the Mau Mau attack and subsequent death of

Mrs Graham, Graham suspects Mwangi had a hand in it. This warrants Mwangi the painful torture he undergoes at the hands of Graham.

The coloniser's "civilising" duty propels him to integrate the local population in his culture so that his stay in the colony is not viewed as an arrogant bother to the natives. This integration can be seen through language. Unlike *Out of Africa*, *The Kitchen Toto*'s Africans and Europeans both try to speak the other's language. The pastor's wife tries her best to speak in English to the policeman and his son, Edward. Although she speaks Kikuyu to all the other Africans in the film, the little English she speaks is reserved for the Europeans. Where she cannot find the English equivalent of what she wants to say, she intentionally uses colloquial Kiswahili, which she is sure the British understand. She calls Edward "Bwana Kidogo" to avoid confusing him by saying "Bwana Mdogo" (Small Master), which is more grammatically correct.[11] On the other hand Mrs Graham, although domineering, brings herself closer to the natives by speaking in Kiswahili. She asks Mugo, her cook to "'koroga' (stir) more" the food before letting it stew. Language therefore becomes a means by which Hook expresses the need for a symbiotic co-existence between the colonial administration and the local people. With the colonised, Mwangi's mother, broken English and the coloniser, Mrs Graham broken Kiswahili, we find a middle ground on which the two intelligibly communicate. It is through this middle-ground language that the coloniser imparts his lifestyle into that of the African. Mugo, the cook, is instructed on how to prepare the master's meal using the new language as seen above.[12]

As a kitchen toto, Mwangi undergoes a cultural transition symbolised by the thorough cleaning he undergoes before Mrs Graham allows him to work for her. The almost silent scene shows Mwangi, stripped naked, being scrubbed with a brush. Mrs Graham ensures that her family is away from the exercise. We see her reprimand Edward, who has been watching Mwangi from a distance. She orders him to get back to the house. The manner in which she does this implies that the dirt from Mwangi might infect her son. After the wash, Mwangi is dressed in new white clothes and his earlier clothes are burnt. As Mugo dresses him, he tells Mwangi: "even your own mother wouldn't recognise you now". He has made contact with the new world and he cannot be the same again, not even to his closest kin. This is his first step towards the coloniser's civilisation. Here, Mwangi and Mugo emerge as hegemonic receivers of the coloniser's mission.

Thus, Harry Hook, like Sidney Pollack, draws from the colonial reservoir of stereotypical characterisation of Africans in film. Colonial British films show African characters who are not well developed, nor given a chance to express their feelings but are structured to further the ideological justification for the imperialists' presence in Africa. Some of these films include *British Palaver* (1926), *Trader Horn* (1931), *Sanders of the River* (1935) and *Rhodes of Africa* (1935). A similar trope can be observed in *The Kitchen Toto* (1985), where two opposing factions of master versus servant come out clearly. In this film, the coloniser is inherently at the centre of power, age notwithstanding. The natives are on the other hand, perpetual servants of these "masters". This explains why Graham is referred to as "Master" while young Edward is called "Small Master". The servants, old or young are referred to by their real names. By showing the African as a consistent servant to the colonial power, the impression created is that it is a plausible and normal occurrence that the African serves the colonial power. Thus, the image of the African in this film is that of a dirty, cruel yet subservient servant, who needs to be enlightened through enculturation into the British lifestyle.

Presentation Of The African Through The Kenyan Filmmaker's Eye

The birth of African filmmaking coincided with political independence of most African countries. It "emerged with the independent movements to liberate African states and coincided with the black consciousness movements of the Diaspora" (Ukadike 1994, 60). Francophone Africa established an early lead in the development of national film industries. This is largely attributed to the continued support received from France in terms of training, financial aid and co-productions. Colonial filmmaking in Africa provided a sound base upon which the newly independent states built their film industries. In Anglophone Africa, only Ghana and Nigeria maintained a steadfast cinematic culture. This was due to their governments' support as well as the presence of the already stable film training institutions in the countries by the time of their independence.[13] East African countries lagged behind in developing national film industries until the 1980s when filmmaking started attracting local attention in the region. In Tanzania, *Arusi ya Mariamu* was made in 1985. In Uganda local productions only came in 1992 with the production of *Feelings Struggle*.[14] Yet in Kenya, films like *Mrembo, Mlevi, Bushtrackers, The Rise and Fall of Idi Amin* and *Kolormask* had been made by the mid1980s.

Given the coincidence, African cinema inevitably joined the other arts in articulating the need for cultural liberation. It therefore emerged as a means of bringing to the fore the African and his lifestyle, which Western films marginalise. Cinema also provided a means of re-writing history. To a large extent, the preceding Western productions as well as the atrocities of the colonial encounter moulded African cinema. It is therefore evident that the concerns of the African film are in many ways similar to those of post-independence African literature. Harris says:

The post-colonial writers' self-appointed mission to forge their countries' national consciousness is largely defined by the Anglocentric portrayal of their culture and people by the earlier British colonial writers. Indeed, the fiction of many Third World writers can only be fully understood through an awareness of its interconnection with earlier British fictional works. Before the emergence of post-colonial fiction, Western readers were given the British view of the empire, and thus, naturally came to see the various colonised lands and peoples as the colonisers saw them. (1994, 179)

Like many national film industries in Africa, the film industry in Kenya has its background in the British colonial administration, where film was used as a tool for education and propaganda. Some of the earliest Kenyan films like *Mrembo* and *Mlevi* were made by independent filmmakers in the 1960s. Later on, *Kolormask* was made using state funds. According to Mukora, "indigenous filmmaking in Kenya began as a counter-colonial discourse similar to that found in the work of such novelists as Meja Mwangi, Grace Ogot, and Ngugi wa Thiong'o" (2003, 227). *Kolormask* aimed at contributing to this debate.

The discussions preceding the production of *Kolormask* reflected some of the resolutions of several manifestos, declarations and resolutions, which had been made concerning African cinema. From the early 1970s, African filmmakers and other prominent cineastes sought to build a common approach to African filmmaking. Between 11th and 13th December 1973, third world filmmakers met in Algiers, Algeria, to deliberate on the possible use of third world cinema as a popular tool of re-making history. They saw cinema as a means of seeking cultural liberation and progress. Solidarity in terms of co-productions among the third world countries was viewed as a means by which the countries would express "anti-imperialist solidarity" (Cham and Bakari 1996, 23).

Adopted at the second Féderation Panafricaine des Cinéastes (FEPACI) in Algiers in January 1975, the Algiers Charter on African Cinema observed that cinema has an important role in the development of third world countries and recognised the capability of cinema to educate, inform and raise consciousness among the masses. It proposed that for African cinema to accomplish these, it has a duty to question the image the Africans have of themselves and their position in global society. The charter called upon individual governments to "take a leading role in building a national cinema" (Bakari and Cham 1996, 26)

Kolormask criticises the cultural alienation that has its roots in the colonial contact between Kenya and Britain in the nineteenth century. John Litodo, a young Kenyan, marries Eliza, a British-born American woman, when he goes to study in London. While in London, he adopts a British lifestyle to ease his stay in the foreign land. The couple relocates to Kenya when John completes his studies. Their two children, Toby and Susan, are already grown up when John realises how withdrawn from his people he has become. Suddenly, John and Eliza's differences magnify as John finds it necessary to trace his way back to his cultural roots.

As seen in the Western films, the colonised is generally portrayed as a silent observer of events and perpetrator of the "master's" desires. They are viewed as lesser beings with whom the coloniser/settler does not freely mix. The Kenyan film positions the African to closely interact with the West as seen in John. John and Eliza's happy life in London, seen through flashback, suggests the acceptance of their marriage in that society. This can be compared to the dramatic scene in *Out of Africa* where Denys discovers that his fellow British settler has secretly married Mariammu, a Somali woman with whom he has been living for five years. This shocks many settlers who consider this kind of mixing unacceptable. As for John and Eliza, the spectator is convinced that their marriage was based on genuine love. Eliza reminisces:

John you were such a beautiful lover! And the nights, Ah! But now look at you. Lying there in bed like a log. Just like a piece of dead wood. When I think of those early days in London—they were so sweet and John, so handsome and strong, black and beautiful. What happened on the road? What happened to our love?

Kolormask is an example of the African films that attempt to redress the inaccurate and incomplete portrait of Africans and their culture. The films tend to move the indigenous characters from scenery backdrops to the foreground while the Western characters find new positions in the background. In *Kolormask*, the story revolves equally around John and Eliza. This enables a better development of the African characters hence the viewer gets to understand him/her more.

Kolormask counters Western films' portrayal of the African as an isolated figure. It does this by defining a character in relation to the people around him/her rather than as the solitary African servant. Presenting the characters together with their extended family and community at large helps the spectator to understand the character better. The spectator's knowledge of the character is, therefore, based upon several relations between the character and his entourage, what he thinks about them and how he treats their beliefs. For example, John is anchored in his extended family. His interaction with relatives, friends, employees and his immediate family all work together in explaining to the spectator what kind of a person John is. For instance, through his conversation with his girlfriend, Dorothy, we come to understand that he does not have a problem with white people, but with his wife's disgusting philosophies.

Kolormask looks at the individual characteristics of man. This goes beyond the colour-mask that creates a rift between peoples of different racial categories in *Out of Africa* and *The Kitchen Toto*. The vices are criticised in general, no matter who commits them. The fact that Eliza (whose behaviour is most condemned) is European does not automatically make her the perpetrator of these acts. John, who doubles as the filmmaker's mouthpiece, as well as the most offended by Eliza, says:

> I am not anti-white. No! My doctrine is simple. All human beings are equal irrespective of colour, creed or even race. You see, people talk of colour, colour, colour...but no! The colour of the skin is not the most important thing, you know. Scientifically, we are all human beings. The colour of the skin does not control our brains.

Sao Gamba justifies this position by presenting to us Susan and Toby, who are mixed race but hold totally opposing views about their identity. Toby believes he is African while Suzy is convinced she is too "civilised" to be an African. She asks her brother to remove his clothes and jump into the forest if he feels like being an African. Suzy's worldview is a replica of her mother's. Gamba, therefore, condemns these worldviews and not the race of their perpetrators.

This is further heightened when we examine Agnes's position, which greatly contrasts with Eliza's. Agnes is a European woman who married into John's village. Although we do not see Agnes' husband, people like Auntie Maria appreciate her respect for the community's customs. Agnes believes that "Africans are real people" and that one just needs to understand their philosophy about life. The Wilson family, although of African descent, are fully metamorphosed into the Western lifestyle.[15] Their views about Africans are similar to Eliza's. Eliza admires the Wilsons so much that she even asks John why they cannot live like the Wilsons. Incidentally, we see roles dramatically changing from what we observe in the colonial films that were initially shown to Africans. The Africans' admiration and awe towards Western life no longer follows the neatly stipulated conventions seen in the Western films. With Agnes and the Wilsons shifting positions, *Kolormask* dismantles such social frontiers, a common observation in postcolonial reading[16].

In describing a "good African film," Nyamwaya et al. say that the famed Ghanaian production, *Love Brewed in the African Pot* was such a success because "Africans enjoy and associate with films that relate with their social environment" (n.d.,13). *Kolormask*, therefore, depicts the situation of the post-independence elite in Kenya. The subject matter revolves around an experience many Kenyans have witnessed in their day-to-day lives. For Kenyans looking towards the West for their tertiary education, and the consequent interracial marriages that are sometimes disturbed by a culture-clash, John and Eliza are part of society. The Wilsons who despise their traditional ways of life after a close mingle with the outside world as well as the Tobies and the Susans, caught up in an identity quagmire, all provide a mirror to the society in which the film is set.

Kinyanjui's *The Battle of the Sacred Tree* tells the story of Mumbi, a young woman who finds it impossible to continue with her marriage to a tyrant living in Nairobi. She decides to quit once and for all and go back to her "backward and primitive" village in Githunguri to live with her poor family. She realises that she needs a source of income. Her request to join a local Christian Mother's Union, hoping to participate in the union's income-generating activities meets stern rejection. The women cannot mix with her since she has failed to keep her marriage. The women find this unacceptable in Christianity. Mumbi's daughter, Thoni, requires school fees yet her mother has no source of income. The pressure gets too much for Mumbi to resist. As a result, she opts to become a barmaid in a local pub in order to meet her needs.

At the same time, the Mother's Union wages war against all the "evils" in the village. They are out to "carry out the work of the Lord". Their radical Christianity is at war with almost every activity going on in the village. They fight the pub, where Mumbi works, and all its patrons. They see Mumbi as a failure, who should not be allowed to mix with "upright" families. They believe that Mumbi's traditional herbalist father, and the sacred *Mugumo* tree, are propagators of "backwardness" in their community. This Manichean clash of interests is solved when the mothers decide to bring the tree down on their own, only to face the wrath of the gods.

Wanjiru Kinyanjui's personal conviction to make a film that presents a more authentic picture of Africa ends in much the same way as Sao Gamba's *Kolormask*.[17] In *The Battle of the Sacred Tree*, Kinyanjui light-heartedly presents a scenario similar to the clash witnessed in *Kolormask*. She employs satire to depict the conflict between the radical Christianity espoused by the women's union and the traditional African culture in a lighter manner.

Two sides emerge in the film. The Kanyore Christian Women's Union are out to wipe out any form of "primitivism" in the village. On the other hand, the rest of the village finds the women too antagonistic towards the so-called "backward ways". The latter group has come to realise that the Euro-Christian dismissal of African religious practices is baseless and closely linked to the colonial process. A shopkeeper tells one of the Christian women who asks him to support the cutting of the tree that he has never read anywhere in the bible against a tree Viewing *Mugumo* (the Sacred Tree) as a symbol of sin is not based upon biblical teachings. Like John in *Kolormask*, the shopkeeper shows the viewer that he is indeed capable of making an informed choice between what is good for him and what he does not need. He has chosen to be a Christian but not to interfere with his ancestral traditions represented by the *Mugumo*.[18]

Kolormask and *The Battle of the Sacred Tree* concur with Diawara's narrative styles as reviewed at the beginning of this chapter. The two films exhibit a "return to the source" and social realist techniques in their attempt at reclaiming the negative portrayal of the African in Western films. In so doing, the two come out as films whose directors heeded the call by a pioneer African film critic, Tahar Cheriaa, that "your cinema shall be a militant cinema, it shall be first and foremost a cultural action with social...value, or it shall be nothing" (see Ngangura 1996, 61).[19]

The two films tend to overemphasise the superiority of the pre-colonial African way of life, painting the colonial centre and its reminders as the backdrop through which the significance of the formerly marginalised African practices is stressed. In *The Battle of the Sacred Tree* for example, Mzee's medicine triumphs over tablets that the patient asks for. The patient believes that Mzee's herbs are useless. On recovering, he goes to the open market, proclaiming the power of Mzee's medication. This is an inversion with which a contemporary viewer may not easily identify. For a film that only reached the market in 2005, ten years after its release, it is difficult to expect the viewer to incorporate the use of traditional medicine when the "tablets" are at his/her disposal. For a majority of Kinyanjui's audience, given the time between the film's release and its availability it becomes unrealistic.

For *Kolormask*, drawing the viewer's attention to the importance of funeral and initiation rites as an African way of life is easily debatable. African, in fact, Kenyan communities are so diversified that presenting how one community treats death or initiation does not reflect how a majority of the communities treat the same. This makes Gamba's depiction of the processes and the importance attached to each stage of the rites unrepresentative of what happens in African communities. These variations are not only present within inter-communal boundaries but are also found in the intra-communal spaces that continue to widen owing to spatial movements that characterise former colonies.

Although *Kolormask*, through John, claims not to be racist, it reveals some conscious attempts by the director, who doubles as the scriptwriter, to relocate the former coloniser to the periphery. Eliza is ridiculed and people like John's relatives, Dorothy, the maidservant and Toby all question her position. We see a similar questioning of the former colonial centre in the restaurant scene, where the minister and his friends wonder why the waiter overlooks their presence, while serving the Europeans with much attention to detail. At this point, the film tries to overtly negate the perception of this centre as the absolute authority as seen in the Western films in this study. Bhabha asks, in "Commitment to Theory":

Can the aim of freedom or knowledge be the simple inversion of the relation of oppressor oppressed, margin periphery, negative image and positive image? Is our only way out of such dualism the espousal of an implacable oppositionality or the invention of an originary counter-myth of radical purity? (1994, 111)

Such inversions run the risk of reproducing the very racism that they were designed to combat. This study has seen that the colonial representation of the African was bound to gain Western superiority. For other Western filmmakers, it aimed at fulfilling their audiences' desire hence raise box office collection. For the post independent filmmaker like Gamba, such militant cinema that may not even receive keen interest from the local audience may not be beneficial, even more so at a time when anti-colonialism was slowly giving way to the globalisation process.

As seen earlier, the two films also fit well with Diawara's description of the social realist style in African cinema. Such films usually question social plausibility of the African in Western films, casting the African as the person sinned against hence the need for the filmmakers to provide a more honest re-presentation of the same. The question of truthfulness in representation remains rather contested as it depends on the filmmaker's spatio-temporal position as well as his/her point of view as s/he approaches the object of representation. Using such a moralistic approach only "casts the question as simply one of errors and distortions as if the truth of a community were unproblematic, transparent and easily accessible, and lies about that community easily unmasked" (Stam 2000, 276). It can be argued that the Western filmmaker, coming from the outside, portrays the African from an outsider's standpoint. For the colonial cinema, other than the vested economic interests at stake, could also have been presenting the society as it seemed to be from the coloniser's point of view. A post-independent portrayal coming from an insider is definitely bound to be different.

Bhabha says that the postcolonial world is culturally and historically hybrid (Bhabha 1994). This gives the post-independent Kenyan filmmaker an extra task; of having to redefine the African he wants to re-present.

The outsider's African has surely changed due to the historical processes like colonisation which have had a direct and inevitable impact on the way of life of the African today. Even for the outsiders like Pollack and Hook, who share time space with the Kenyan filmmakers, their exotic view of the African cannot have the same results as the insider's might. An outsider's record may be faulty but cannot reflect an insider's. The Kenyan filmmaker's re-presentation of the African in film may only add to the Western filmmaker's observation but cannot replace it due to the shifting paradigms of their different observations about the same object.

The situation is even worsened by the African filmmakers' tendency to move between the global South and North as the distinct locations of the (ex) coloniser and (ex) colonised. Sao Gamba and Wanjiru Kinyanjui number among the many African filmmakers to study their art in the developed countries. *Kolormask* and *The Battle of the Sacred Tree* are products of skills acquired in Poland and Germany respectively. Such movements make the viewer question the authenticity of their "authentic" view of the African. This study agrees with Trinh Minh-ha's position in "Outside In Inside Out" that "the moment the insider steps out from the inside, she is no longer a mere insider. She necessarily looks in from the outside while also looking out from the inside" (1989, 145). From the filmmakers' journeys between the two worlds, their worldviews become an amalgam of the multiple cultures with which they interact. This raises another concern about the credence of their re-presentation of the African compared to that of the locally trained filmmakers.

Even in the hands of the Kenyan filmmakers, the image of the African remains ambiguous. This is reflected in Paulin Soumanou Vieyra's "African Cinema: Solidarity and Difference" (1994). He associates the varied nature of African cinema with film directors' disparate backgrounds in terms of training and individual preferences.[20] With such differences, it is evident "there no longer is a position of authority from which one can definitely judge the verisimilitude value of the representation." Trinh says "the questioning subject, even if s/he is an insider is no more authentic and has no more authority on the subject matter" (Trinh 1989, 146). The call for African filmmakers to work against imperial oppression through cinema becomes even blurrier in the age of independent filmmaking in Kenya.

Even as Gamba and Kinyanjui's works attempt to improve on the colonial portrayal of the African through the two films, the films themselves give a contradiction of this. Gamba's attempt to elevate John to a decision-maker and breadwinner in his family is pegged on the source of that superiority; John is introduced to the spectator at a point when he has been successfully weaned into Western education and professionalism. This depicts London as an admirable "centre," where economic success and subsequent power is attainable. Gamba, therefore, hints at a more optimistic image of the coloniser than expected, given the pre-meditated need to underscore African personality and culture.

The film also ridicules the independence of the African from the colonial regime. In the restaurant scene, the post-independence minister who has taken over political leadership from the coloniser fails to acquire the respect that he expects to come with the position. The waiter neglects the minister's table and gives personalised service to the European patrons. The minister and his friends continuously summon the waiter for over fifteen minutes and are always told to wait. The waiter only serves them after being told that the patron is a minister and after the minister demands dialogue with the manager of the restaurant. The next scene moves to a nearby table where a white customer talks about the false independence of the colonies. This scene seems to mock the very self-governance that it tries to praise. The psychological imprint of the colonial encounter is thus highlighted through the actions of the waiter.

Similarly, *The Battle of the Sacred Tree* makes fun of the Christian Women's union. The women's understanding of Christianity does not help them or the society they live in. The viewer may wonder whether laughing at the women gives the African audience a better understanding of self than watching Mwangi in *The Kitchen Toto*. As observed in this section, the question emerging is, therefore, not that of merely "correcting" the images the Western films show of the African. Sometimes, the image of the colonised in his/her own creative works may betray his quest for a better portrayal by the coloniser. Judgement of the image is also dependent on the position of the viewer and what informs his viewing. His/her socio-political, historical or even racial background could contrive a viewer's interpretation of a film.

Conclusion

The director/scriptwriters of the two films are among the filmmakers who hold the view that one of the roles of the African filmmaker is to present to his audience an African with whom they can identify. This is opposed to the continued negative portrayal of the African in Western films.

This view is observed throughout the two films. In trying to meet this objective, the films adopt two of the tendencies that have been commonly used by African filmmakers in trying to re-present Africa: the return to the source and realist tradition. Their portrayal of the African is however questioned. The films give contradicting images, which leave the ownership of authority and authenticity of re-presentation ambiguous.

Thus, one cannot assume an automatic connection between control over representation and the production of positive images. The fact that the oppressed—be it the colonised in postcolonialism, women in Feminist theory, homosexuals in Queer theory—did not have an ultimate say on the manner in which their oppressors— colonialism, patriarchy and cisnormative structures of society respectively—present them should not mean that given the powers, the oppressed are bound to give a positive representation of themselves.

References

Achebe, Chinua. 1975. *Morning Yet on Creation Day.* London: Heinemann.

Ahmed, A. Akbar. 1995. *Postmodernism and Islam: Predicament and Promise.* London: Routledge.

Anyinefa, Kofi. 2000. "Postcolonial Post-modernity in Henry Lopes' *Le Pleurer-Rire*". In *The Post-colonial Condition of African Literature*, edited by Daniel Gover, John Conteh-Morgan and Jane Bryce, pp. 5-22. Trenton: Africa World Press.

Ashcroft, Bill, Gareth Griffiths and Helen Tiffin. 1989. *The Empire Writes Back: Theory and Practice in Post-colonial Literatures.* London: Routledge.

Atieno-Odhiambo, 1971. "The Historical Sense and Creative Literature". In *Black Aesthetics*, edited by Andrew Gurr and Pio Zirimu. Nairobi: East African Literature Bureau.

Bahri, D. and M. Vasudeva. 1996. *Between the Lines: South Asians and Postcoloniality.* Philadelphia: Temple University.

Bakari, Imruh and Mbye Cham. eds. 1996. *African Experiences of Cinema.* London: British Film Institute.

Bakupa, B. Kanyinda. 2004. "Film in Africa, Africa in Film: Challenging Stereotypes." A Chapter Presented at Africa Cine Week, Nairobi.

Balogun, Francoise. 2004. "Blooming Videoeconomy: The Case of Nigeria". In *Focus on African Films*, edited by Francoise Pfaff, pp. 173-84. Bloomington and Indianapolis: Indiana University Press.

Barlet, Olivier. 2000. *African Cinemas: Decolonizing the Gaze.* Translated by Chris Turner. London: Zed Books.

Bettetini, Giafranco. 1973. *The Language and Technique of the Film.* The Hague: Mouton.

Bhabha, Homi. 1994. *The Location of Culture.* London: Routledge.

—.1994. "Commitment to Theory". In *Questions of Third Cinema*, edited by Jim Pines and Paul Willeman, pp. 90-110. London: British Film Institute.

Bjorn, Lindgren. 2001." Representing the Past in the Present". In *Encounter Images in the Meetings between Africa and Europe*, edited by Mai Palmberg, pp. 121-34. Uppsala: Nordic Africa Institute.

Carter, Cynthia and Stuart Allan. 2000. "If it Bleeds, it Leads: Ethical Questions about Popular Journalism". In *Ethics and Media Culture: Practices and Representations*, edited by David Berry, pp. 132-53. Oxford: Focal Press.

Césaire, Aimé. 1994. "From Discourse on Colonialism". In *Colonial Discourse and Postcolonial Theory: A Reader*, edited by Patrick Williams and Laura Chrisman, pp. 172- 80. Essex: Pearson Education Limited.

Cham, Mbye. 1996. "Introduction". In *African Experiences of Cinema*, edited by Imruh Bakari and Mbye Cham, pp. 1-14. London: British Film Institute.

Chemjor, Walter K. *"Style and Ideology in Colonial Writing: A Study of Karen Blixen's* Out of Africa." (Unpub.) Mphil. Thesis. Eldoret: Moi university, 1998.

ComMatters Ltd. *African Cine Week Kenya*. Nairobi: FCCC, 2003.

Darwin, Charles. 1859. *The Origin of Species by Means of Natural Selection*. London: John Murray.

Diawara, Manthia. 1992. *African Cinema: Politics and Culture*. Bloomington and Indianapolis: Indiana University Press.

Dinesen, Isak. 1937. *Out of Africa* London: Putnam.

Dominique, Nasta. 1991. *Meaning in Film: Relevant Structures in Soundtrack and Narrative*. Bern: Peter Lang.

Eke, N. Maureen, Kenneth W. Harrow and Emmanuel Yewah.eds. 2000. *African Images: Recent Studies and Text in Cinema*. No. New Jersey: Africa World Press.

Ellerson, Beti. 2000.*Sisters of the Screen*. New Jersey: Africa World Press.

Fanon, Frantz. 1952. *Black Skin White Masks*. Translated by Charles Markmann (1973). St Albans: Paladin.

—.1967. *The Wretched of the Earth*. Translated by Constance Farrington. Harmondsworth: Penguin.

Frost, Richard. 1997. *Race Against Time: Human Relations and Politics in Kenya Before Independence*. Nairobi: Trans Africa Press.

Gandhi, Leela. 1998. *Postcolonial Theory: A Critical Introduction*. New York: Columbia University.

Giannetti, L. 1990. *Understanding Movies* (5th ed.). New Jersey: Prentice.

Gilman, L. Sander. 1985. *Difference and Pathology: Stereotypes of Sexuality, Race and Madness*. Ithaca: Cornell University.

Gover, Daniel, John Conteh-Morgan and Jayne Bryce. eds. 2000. *The

Postcolonial Condition of African Literature. New Jersey: Africa World Press.

Griffiths, Garreth. 2000. *African Literatures in English: East and West.* Harlow: Longman.

Harris, Michael. 1994. *Outsiders & Insiders: Perspectives of Third World Culture in British and Post-colonial Fiction.* New York: Peter Lang.

Kurtz, Roger. 1998. *Urban Obsessions, Urban Fears: The Postcolonial Kenyan Novel.* Trenton: Africa World Press.

Lindfors, Bernth. 2001. "Hottentot, Bushman, Kaffir: The Making of Racist Stereotypes in 19th Century Britain". In *Encounter Images in the Meetings between Africa and Europe,* edited by Mai Palmberg, pp. 54-75. Uppsala: Nordic Africa Institute.

Lye, John. 1997. "Some Issues in Postcolonial Theory" www.brocku.ca/english/courses/4170/postcol.php. Last updated 30th April, 2008.

Maasik, Sonia and Jack Solomon. 2000. "Popular Signs: or Everything You've Always Known about American Culture (But Nobody Asked)". In *Signs of Life in the USA: Readings on Popular Culture for Writers,* edited by Sonia Maasik and Jack Solomon, pp.1-19. Boston/New York: Bedford/St Martin's.

Mgbejume, Onyero. 1989. *Film in Nigeria: Development, Problems and Promise.* Nairobi: African Council on Communication Education.

Minh-ha, T. Trinh. 1994. "Outside In Inside Out". In *Questions of Third Cinema,* edited by Jim Pines and Paul Willeman, 113-49. London: British Film Institute.

Mishra, Vijay and Bob Hodge. 1994. "What is Post(-)colonialism?" In *Colonial Discourse and Post-colonial Theory: A Reader,* edited by Patrick Williams and Laura Chrisman, pp. 276-90. Essex: Pearson Education Limited.

Moggi, Paola and Roger Tessier. 2001. "Media Status Report: Kenya". Nairobi: Tangaza College.

Mukora, W.B. 2005. "African Cinema", in www.pacweb.org accessed on 20th October 2005.

Mukora, W Beatrice. 2003. "Beyond Tradition and Modernity: Representations of Identity in Two Kenyan Films." In *Women Filmmakers Refocusing,* edited by Jacqueline Levitin, Judith Plessis and Valerie Raoul. Pp. 219-28. New York: Routledge.

Mungai, Anne. 1997. Interview with Beti Ellerson, Ougadougou.

Nacify, Hamin. 1994. "Mediaworks' Representation of the Other: The

Case of Iran." In *Questions of Third Cinema*, edited by Jim Pines and Paul Willeman, pp. 227-39. London: British Film Institute.

Nangoli, Musamaali. 1986. *No More Lies about Africa: Here is the Truth From an African*. East Orange, NJ: African Heritage publishers.

Ngangura, Mwenze. 1996. "Militancy or Entertainment?" In *African Experiences of Cinema*, edited by Imruh Bakari and Cham Mbye. London: British Film Institute.

Ngayane, Lionel. 1989/1999. "For Africans, with Africans, by Africans" In *Africa on Film* Dossier 10: Africa at the Pictures.

Nyamwaya, S. N. et al. "Evaluation Report: Kenya Film Corporation Ltd" (Undated).

Ochieng', Philip. 1992. *I Accuse the Press: An Insider's View of the Media and Politics in Africa*. Nairobi: Initiatives.

Odari, H. Masumi. 2003. "Self Identity—Reflections on Yusuf K. Dawood". *The Nairobi Journal of Literature*. No. 1: 10-14.

Ogot, Bethwell A. and William. R. Ochieng'.eds.1996. *Decolonization and Independence in Kenya: 1940-93*. Nairobi: East African Educational Publishers.

Olago, S. O. 2002. *Who Are You, African?* Nairobi: Fotoform.

Parker, Michael and Roger Starkey.1995.eds.*Postcolonial Literatures: Achebe, Ngugi, Desai*. Houndmills: Macmillan.

Pauly, Rebecca M. 1993.*The Transparent Illusion: Image and Ideology in French Text and Film*. New York: Peter Lang.

Pfaff, Francoise.ed.2004. *Focus on African Films*. Bloomington and Indianapolis: Indiana University Press.

Pfister, M. 1991. *The Theory and Analysis of Drama*. Cambridge: Cambridge University Press.

Pieterse, J. Nederveen and Bhikhu Parekh. 1995. "Shifting Imaginaries: Decolonization, Internal Decolonization, Postcoloniality". In *The Decolonization of Imagination: Culture, Knowledge and Power*, edited by J. N. Pieterse and Bhikhu Parekh, pp. 1-19. London: Zed Books.

Pines, Jim and Paul Willeman.eds. 1994. *Questions of Third Cinema*. London: British Film Institute.

Ross, Karen. 2000. "In Whose Image? TV Criticism and Black Minority Viewers". In *Ethnic Minorities and the Media*, edited by Simon Cottle. Buckingham: Open University Press.

Said, Edward. 1978. *Orientalism*. New York: Routledge and Kegan Paul.

Simiyu, Barasa. *A History of Film in Kenya: 1909-2009*. Nairobi: Simbavision/Twaweza Communications.

Sipalla, Florence. 2004. "Dangerous Affair: Narrating Popular Experiences in Kenya." Unpublished MA Thesis. Johannesburg: University of Witwatersrand.

Stam, Robert. 2000. *Film Theory: An Introduction*. Massachusetts: Blackwell.

Ukadike, Frank Nwachukwu. 1994. *Black African Cinema*. Chicago: University of Chicago Press.

Vera, Yvonne. 2001. "A Voyeur's Paradise...Images of Africa". In *Encounter Images in the Meetings between Africa and Europe*, edited by Mai Palmberg, pp. 115-20. Uppsala: Nordic Africa Institute.

Vieyra, Paulin Soumanou. 1994. "African Cinema: Solidarity and Difference". In *Questions of Third Cinema*, edited by Jim Pines and Paul Willeman, pp. 195-98. London: British Film Institute.

Wa Gacheru, Margaretta. 1994. "Distribution: East Africa". In *Africa Film and TV*. Harare: Z Promotions.

Wa Thiong'o, Ngugi. 1977. Homecoming: *Essays on African and Caribbean Literature, Culture and Politics*. London: Heinemann.

—. 1986. *Decolonising the Mind: The Politics of Language in African Literature*. Nairobi: East African Educational Publishers.

Primary Films Cited

Gamba, Sao. *Kolormask*. 1985.

Hook, Harry. *The Kitchen Toto*. 1985.

Kinyanjui, Wanjiru. *The Battle of the Sacred Tree*. 1994.

Pollack, Sydney. *Out of Africa*. 1987.

Endnotes

i. Decolonization runs through not only the creative works but also the critical writings of many post-colonial authors in Africa. Some of these include writers like Ngugi wa Thiong'o (1972 and 1981); Chinua Achebe (1975); Olivier Barlet (2000) Kanyinda Bakupa (2004) and historians, Ochieng' and Ogot (1996) among others.

ii. Mukora, W.B. in "African Cinema", www.pacweb.org 2005.

iii. One good example of such is the collection of essays in Eke et al. (2000) *African Images: Recent Studies and Text in Cinema.*

iv. Kinyanjui and Muigai in Ellerson (2000). Also see Mungai with Ellerson (1997).

v. Interview with Beti Ellerson at FESPACO. Ouagadougou, Burkina Faso, 1997.

vi. Interview with Beti Ellerson in *Sisters of the Screen* (2000).

vii. One such writer is wa Thiong'o (1972) who sees the need for us to view Africa in three broad phases: Pre-colonial, colonial and post-colonial Africa. He describes the last phase as a period of Africa's search for her "true self-image." This search indicates that Africa's both internal and external pressures have caused her cultural needs and subsequently her cultural image to change during her development. Ali Mazrui in his documentary film *The Africans* expresses the need to understand Africa through her history, which has been influenced by several contacts (with both Asia and the west), giving Africa a "triple heritage." This has ultimately necessitated her search for her true image.

viii. Other scholars who share similar sentiments include David Kerr 1995, Louis Tyson 1999, Yvonne Vera 2001, Bernth Lindfors 2001 and Lindgren Bjorn 2001.

ix. This was founded in 1935 by Major L. A. Notcutt. The programme had a mandate to educate adult Africans to change and adapt to new ways of life, prescribed by the British colonisers. It also had a duty to entertain. Notcutt trained and directed the native actors.

x. These "voices" can be located in the post-independence literary as well as cinematic products of the African states. Most of these works have employed several techniques in attempting to re-present the African, highlighting what is African.

xi. This and all other translations from Kiswahili are mine, unless otherwise indicated.

xii. Although it is currently common to find African men preparing meals, in most African communities, it is more typical for men to distance themselves from the kitchen as it is regarded as women's territory. With the colonial masters employing male cooks and domestic servants the colonised subject is left with no option but to comply since the wages they earn out of such jobs not only provides food for their families but also enables them to pay tax to the colonial government.

xiii. See Lionel Ngayane's "For Africans with Africans by Africans," 1989/1999; Mgbejume, Onyero's *Film in Nigeria: Development, Problems and Promise*, 1989 and Francoise Balogun's "Blooming Videoeconomy: The Case of Nigeria" in Francoise Pfaff (2004).

xiv. From a talk given by the film's director, Ashraf Semwogerere, during a panel group discussion on *The Challenges of Filmmaking in East Africa* at the Second East African Film Congress organised by Amakula, Kampala International Film Festival 2005.

xv. Wilson, an African whose extended family resides in rural Kenya, is married to an African-American woman. The wife refutes the historical relationship between Africans and African-Americans. The Wilsons have so much identified with the Western way of life that they find Wilson's extended family unbelievably backward. According to Nangoli (1986, in his *No More Lies About Africa*, "The mere fact that African people live in the Americas, the West Indies and Europe, having fast been chained and taken against their will to strange lands as captives, does not, in my opinion, remove their link with mother Africa.... " (29). Similarly, Ngugi wa Thiong'o in *Decolonising the Mind*, locates African connections to the four corners of the earth. He says these people are historically linked through biology, culture and struggle. Ngugi believes that the Afro-Americans, for example, share with Africa the same "bio-geographical roots." He therefore refers to the Afro-Americans as "Africans who a few hundred years ago were brutally uprooted from the African continent" (98). He concludes that they both have shared the same past of humiliation and exploitation and they have similar aspirations "for total liberation of all black people in the world." Harris (*Outsiders and Insiders*) and Fanon (*The Wretched of the Earth*) share the same position, referring to this link as the shared history of subjugation which leads its subjects to a common destiny of liberation.

xvi. Kofi Anyinefa, in "Postcolonial Post-modernity" focuses on the similarities in approach between postcolonial and post-modern criticism. One of the areas in which the two share, he says, is on the fact that they both question the social as well as artistic frontiers in a work of art (2000, 15).

xvii. Wanjiru attests to this in Ellerson (2000).

xviii. This assertion is made with regard to the story about the (Kikuyu) tribal origin as narrated in Jomo Kenyatta's book, *Facing Mount Kenya* (1938). In this myth, it is said that at the beginning of time there existed Gikuyu and his wife Mumbi (which means creator or moulder). God enabled them to have nine beautiful daughters, but no son. Since Gikuyu was the first man on earth, there were no other families. So Gikuyu offered sacrifice to the god under a *mugumo* tree after which god provided nine young, handsome men to marry the nine daughters of Gikuyu. The whole community of the Kikuyu tribe sprung out of these nine marriages. *Mugumo* has ever since been viewed as a sacred tree under which the Kikuyu traditionally offered prayers to god (locally called *Ngai*).

xix. Kinyanjui infers her commitment to this call in Ellerson (2000). Gamba is one of the people who wrote the report on Kenyan Cinema which is referred to in this work as Nyamwaya et al. The most memorable impact of this report was the Kenyan Government's support for the production of *Kolormask*.

xx. My use of the expression "African Cinema" is however different from Vieyra's reference to the same in her essay as "African Film". She believes that filmmaking in Africa has not reached the status of being called "a Cinema." Her definition of "cinema" in the same work is not pegged on the process of development but relies on content. She says Cinema includes filmmaking, training, television and all types of films produced within a particular region. This, applied to Africa, concurs with what has been referred to by cinema scholars as African Cinema. Chief Nanga

Chapter Four
Translation and Language Teaching
Margaret S. Amateshe

Introduction

This chapter sets out to discuss the important steps in the teaching of translation. It begins by highlighting what translation entails and the fact that it trains the reader to search for the most appropriate words to convey what is meant. It further focuses on the Relevance theory as an important tool for meaning analysis which can lead to deeper understanding of the meaning of the original text. The chapter also discusses the process of translation that emphasizes the need to analyze, transfer and restructure a message from the source language. It then outlines the steps in the teaching of translation. In so doing, it depicts the need to teach translation in order to render obsolete language barrier and any other language problems that do exist in communication.

This chapter focuses on the types of translation, the Translation Theory, the translation process and the teaching of translation. Basic language teaching methods throughout history have centered on translation and almost all language learning develops out of translation (Duff, 1994). Nida and Taber (1969) state that translation consists of reproducing in the receptor language the closest natural equivalent of the source language message, first in terms of meaning and secondly in terms of style. Munday (2008) defines translation as the result of a text processing activity, by means of which a source language text is transported into a target language text. Between the resultant text in L2 (the target language text) and the source text in L1 (the source language text), there exists a relationship which can be described as a translational or equivalence relation. Cartford (1965) on his part views translation as an operation performed on languages: "a process of substituting a text in one language for a text in another". He argues that the reference to substitution is important, because we do not transfer meaning between languages but merely replace a source language meaning by a target language meaning that can function in the same way in the situation at hand. All the definitions recognize the importance of translation in highlighting both the contrasts and similarities between languages and most importantly, in inter-lingual and ethno-linguistics analysis of languages.

Language and Translation

For a translation to be good, it must render the original meaning of the message accurately, clearly and naturally (Nida, 1959). To do this, it must use the grammar, sentence structure, the lexical and idiomatic expressions of the new language. For example:

ENGLISH	**LUHYA (Kikisa dialect)**
Tractor	irakita
Mobile phone	imobaili
Clinic	ikliniki
Television	Itivi

The source language concept is not lexicalized in the target language but the translation arising has the quality of absoluteness. We know the term but lack the specific meaning in the target language and therefore, opt for the strategy of loan translation. This is a special kind of borrowing which involves a direct translation of the elements of a word into the borrowing language, in order **to accurately transfer** the message of the original text.

Translation goes beyond simply linguistic equivalence of meaning, since in practice, anyone involved in the process must be aware of the paralinguistic implications of the message being conveyed. Obviously, the closer the source language is to the target language, the easier it will be to transfer meaning successfully (Hervey and Higgins, 1992). Difficulties arise through, when the source language and the target language are more distant or when the meaning patterns of the source language differ from the target language, in which case, they are likely to influence target production. For example, when one talks of **'Box'** in English, there are various hyponyms used to specify which type of `Box` one is referring to: **Coffin, Suitcase, Carton box, wooden box etc.** However, the Luhya language (Kikisa dialect) has only the super-ordinate and lacks the specific term for each of the lexical items one may be talking about. The word **`Box`** *(Lisanduku)* is used to refer to all the other types of boxes noted in the English language and this could be because the two languages are distant.

Hatim (2001) states that for translation equivalence to occur, both the source language and target language texts must be relatable to the functionally relevant features of the situation. He views the process of transfer to have been influenced by the following factors:

- Source language and target language code properties, possibilities and limitations
- How reality is perceived and practiced
- Linguistics, stylistics and aesthetic norms
- Translation tradition
- Client specification

Based on the above, the source text is seen as a fundamental element of translation and translation equivalence is achieved within framework of equivalence.

Translation helps us to understand better the influence of one language on another. Since translation involves contrast, it enables us to explore the potential of languages, their strengths and weaknesses. Teachers consider translation to be something boring, pointless, difficult, irrelevant and uncommunicative (Duff, 1994). However, teaching translation helps learners communicate into and from a foreign language. It enables them convey messages across linguistic and cultural barriers. In translation, the original language is often referred to as the source language (SL) or the source text (ST) and the new language of translation as the target language (TL) or the target text (TT). For the purpose of our discussion in this chapter, we shall adopt the abbreviation "SL" for source language and "TL" for target language.

Translation studies have only recently begun to be considered as an independent discipline (Carmen, 1994).Many questions remain unanswered. One which has not received much attention is that connected with the teaching of translation. This chapter attempts to discuss the steps involved in the teaching of translation. However, this cannot be done without first making reference to the theory and process of translation.

The Relevance Theory

The teaching of translation can only be discussed on the backdrop of translation theories that guide the process of translation. As much as it would be prudent to discuss all theories related to translation (Linguistic, Comparative, Cultural, Interpretive, Scopes, Relevance etc), the scope of this chapter cannot allow. We therefore confine ourselves to the Relevance Theory of Communication that was developed by Sperber and Wilson (1986).

In this chapter, we find the Relevance Theory an effective tool in meaning analysis and which can lead to deeper understanding of the meaning of the original text. Gutt (1991) and Zhonggang (2006) state that translation can be accounted for naturally within the Relevance Theory of Communication. That there is no need for a distinct general theory of translation since most kinds of translation can be analyzed as varieties of interpretive use.

According to Sperber and Wilson (1986), the process of communication succeeds because of the principle of relevance. A proposition (statement/utterance) is said to contain optimum relevance when a receptor can interpret it at minimal processing cost within given contextual effects. For instance, if a speaker is saying something and the receptor does not struggle to understand, then s/he gets it as a minimal processing cost. The contextual effects are the evidences in the context that enable the receptor to make the correct inferences. Relevance is the crucial notion that enables people to know which inferences the communicator intended. For example:

Speaker: *Do you mind to take a walk with me?*

Receptor: *I am reading a story book.*

The speaker and the receptor share evidence in the context, though the receptor does not say YES/NO. The shared belief is that taking a walk is good for the health and reading a story book is a healthy pass-time activity too. The relevance is that one who is reading a book cannot take a walk since s/he is equally engaged. Hatim (2001) states that relevance is gained by communication clues which are features built into the text for the purpose of guiding the audience to the intended interpretation. These are phonological, onomatopoeic and figurative expressions among others.

Gutt (1989) saw relevance theory as an effective tool for meaning analysis. In this respect, it can lead to a much deeper understanding of the meaning of the original text. The success of a translation can be judged according to how relevant its contextual effects are and whether receptors are able to access it at minimal processing cost. According to Gerding-Salas (2012), it is important to rely on context to translate because no word in any language has a fixed meaning. A word may be used connotatively or denotatively depending on the context. A translator should understand that meaning is not conveyed through words. A single word in one language often has meaning that requires several words in another.

Relevance Theory, therefore, helps the translator to comprehend not only the meaning of words, sentences and discourse structures but also the symbolic nature of events and the objects that are mentioned in the discourse. The theory is also important in distinguishing between the designative (basic) and the associative (interpretive) meanings. It also emphasizes that everything about a message carries meaning. Proceeding from the discussion above, this chapter finds the relevance Theory adequate in discussing the teaching of translation.

The Translation process

The process of translation comprises in its essence the whole secret of human understanding of the world and social communication (Biguenet and Schulte, 1989). Translation must reproduce the whole by trying to put the particulars of a text into focus and interaction. According to Nida and Taber (1969), translation takes place in three stages namely: analysis, transfer and restructuring. Nida (1975) posits that the translator first analyses the message of the SL into its simplest and structural clearest forms. The translator then transfers it at this level in the TL that is most appropriate for the audience s/he intends to reach. The model below summarizes this process:

Figure 3.1: The Translation process

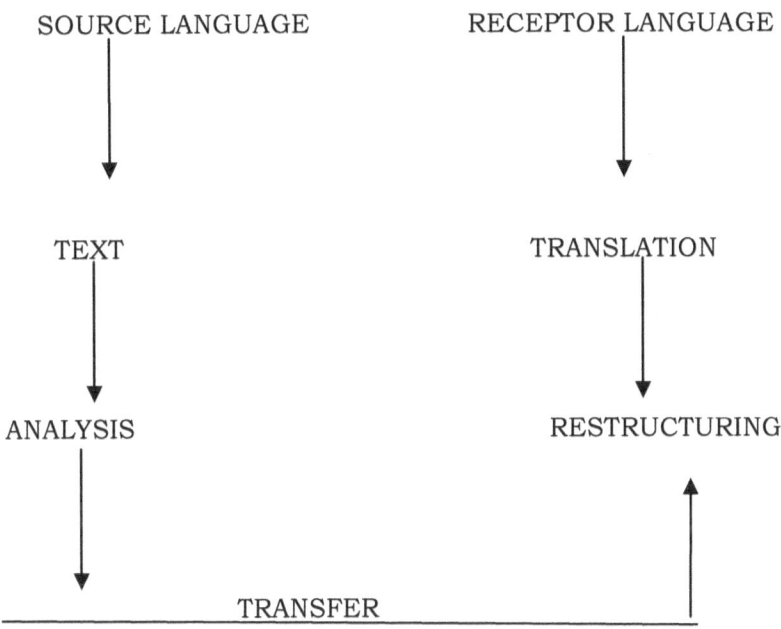

Source:Nida, A. Eugene (1975): *Language Structure and Translation*.

The model illustrates that what is important to be transferred in translation is the content of the text and not the form. Nida's model of translation has come to be inextricably linked with the notion of dynamic equivalence which also involves regulating redundancy in order to facilitate comprehension, and substituting more appropriate TL and cultural material for less accessible SL items (Hatim,2001).

Nida and Taber (1969) claim that translation from one language to the other is made easier by the codability of the linguistic items involved. Something is said to be codable if it falls within the scope of readily available terms used in a particular language. The higher the codability of concepts in the TL, the higher the translatability. Dra (2010) affirms that the reconstruction of the translation process leads to the formulation of the methods that are fundamental, not only to the practice of translation but also to the act of reading and interpreting. Whatever the difficulty in the translation process, procedures must aim at the essence of the message and faithfulness to the meaning of the SL text being transferred to the TL text.

In this section, we have shown that understanding the translation process is key in being able to teach translation and for the translators to be able to comprehend the task involved in translation. Understanding the process will enable the teacher and learners adopt the most effective strategies in their translation exercises.

Teaching Translation

According to Gerding-Salas (2012), the aim of translation is to serve as a cross-cultural bilingual communication vehicle among people. She further states that in the past few decades, this activity has developed because of rising international trade, increased migration, globalization, the recognition of linguistic minorities and the expansion of the mass media and Technology. For this reason, the translator plays an important role as a bilingual or multi-lingual cross-cultural transmitter of culture and truths by attempting to interpret concepts and speech in a variety of texts as faithfully and accurately as possible. Bassnett (1980) posits that over 60% of the world is bi- or multi-lingual, so translation is an everyday activity for many people, with extremely practical applications. It is therefore important to teach translation and encourage learners to develop useful, applicable techniques to deal with it.

According to Samudra (1993) as cited by Dra (2010), a balance between theory and practice should be kept in the teaching of translation, although it can lean a little bit on practice. This is because it is practice that actually produces a good translator. In other words, there is need for students to practice translating as much as possible, by analyzing texts in the SL, restructuring and evaluating the translation in the TL.

For example, a warning sign such as *"Trespassers will be persecuted"* could simply be translated into Kiswahili as *"usipite hapa."* This communicates the strong warning of the English Version. The gist of it is to conceptualize the picture and then translate in the simplest form.

The first point to consider in choosing work for the students is their background, expectation, experience, knowledge about translation and interest (Dra 2010). If the teacher knows about students' knowledge and experience in translation, s/he will be in a position to choose text assignment for them, basing on the level of difficulty. If they have no experience in translation, then simple texts should be chosen to start them off. For example, lexical texts as opposed to idiomatic expressions or sentence structures would make a good starting point. Knowing the students' interest will be useful in choosing text assignment that suits their interest. Translation is first a sense–making exercise. The translator must understand and make sense of the materials s/he is translating, before converting it to TL. It is in this sense-making process where the translator's knowledge, social background and personal experience come into play.

There is need to explain to the students the main theory and the process of translation, pointing out that what is important to be transferred in translation is the content of the text and not the form. That is, within the relevance theory, everything about a message carries meaning. The theory would guide the learners in comprehending not only the meaning of words, sentence and discourse structures but also the symbolic nature of events and the objects that are mentioned in the discourse. For instance, an utterance such as, *"I have a million things to do"* is interpretively understood to mean, *"I am extremely busy"*. The two utterances share contextual implications in a certain context. The first utterance represents the second utterance due to their interpretive resemblance.

Knowledge of the process of translation would assist students analyze the message in the SL text, transfer and restructure in the TL text to the level that is most appropriate for the intended audience. For example, the Luhya (Kikisa dialect) idiom *"Atetekhana yayia ameno"* could simply be translated into English as *"Hurry hurry has no blessings"*. Adapting a word-to word rendering could completely distort the meaning of the idiom as it would read, *"The one hurrying burnt his teeth"*, which is not the equivalent of the idiom in the SL in terms of meaning. A paraphrase gives us a close to an equivalent translation as illustrated above. Students therefore need to be aware of the equivalent effect of what they translate. That is, whether the effect of the TL will be equal to that of the SL by reflecting accurately the meaning of the original text.

According to Duff (1994) translation should begin with short texts (such as a story from a news chapter) for reading and discussion to save time. Short texts train students to transfer the content of a text from SL to TL. The text should be short, so that the students are able to remember it after reading or listening to it once. These texts must be interesting, relevant and as far as possible, authentic. They should also reflect students' needs and be appropriate to their level. Besides, they should represent full range of style and register. This will be of great help to the students if they face real world texts and tasks. In addition, texts must be chosen according to previously defined objectives for translation practice, taking into account the degree of difficulty of the texts(semantic, cultural, stylistic etc), the topic of the specific knowledge area (Political, economic etc.), the translation problem to be encountered and soon.

Translation can be a highly effective way of drawing learner's attention to the linguistic, semantic and pragmatic features of the TL. For instance, the Luhya word *"Ndakhusasaka"* to mean *"I am extremely mad"* may lack an equivalent in English. Translated literally, it would read,*"I will beat you to pup."* However, this translation ignores the expressing equivalent meaning and therefore fails to realize the equivalent in TL. The word *"Ndakhusasaka"* is emotionally loaded and the translation *"I am extremely mad/angry"* is more adequate.

The translation exercise can take the form of a few sentences to be translated into the TL, or TL sentences to be translated into the SL (Gerding-Salas, 2012). However, a short passage is usually much more stimulating and practical rather than a list of sentences with little context. The teacher can select material to illustrate particular aspects of language and structures the students have difficulty with. By working through these difficulties in the mother tongue, the students can see the link between the language grammar and usage (Duff, 1994).

All acts of translation begin with a thorough investigation of the reading process. It is important for the students to first read through the longer texts assisted by the teacher, since incorrect comprehension of a text considerably decreases the quality of translation. They should be able to identify the source, the norm, the type of text, the register, the style and the readership of the text selected. The students should read the whole text at least twice. The first reading will be comprehensive and general, to become acquainted with the topic and to understand the original, always bearing in mind that meaning is context-determined (Gerding-Salas, 2012). The second reading must be a "deep" reading, placing emphasis on items where translation problems may appear. When doing this "reading with translation intention," students should first underline unknown terms and then they should mentally confront potential translation difficulties in the text with suitable translation procedures. In the translation process, thinking grows out of the situation within a text; it is not brought to the text from the outside (Biguenet and Schulte, 1989).

Newmark (1995) states that translation is for discussion. Texts chosen should thus stimulate interaction leading to active class discussion. The discussions, carried out in groups or in pairs, give all the students a chance to be heard, to test their ideas against the others, to listen and compare. In translation, there is hardly any right answer but there are a lot of wrong ones. Doing all the work individually and writing is not necessary. What the students need is to work in pairs or groups for oral discussion. The role of the teacher is to listen to the translations, explain important points which are not covered by the students, especially the ones concerning theory or guidelines of translation.

According to Gerding-Salas (2012), students can be asked to compare different versions of translation written by them. The teacher prepares two short texts for translation from SL to TL. Individually, each student writes a quick translation of their text into TL after which they compare their translations and discuss the differences between their TL versions. They can then discuss different aspects of the text and finally write in pairs or groups a new "ideal" translation. Through this activity, the students' awareness of the skills of translation and the differences between their own language and target language are raised. It encourages them to think about aspects of context and to pay attention to the "social" meaning of the words and phrases which they select.

Dra (2010) states that if students are accustomed to discussing translation problems in class, it is likely that they are more critical in evaluating their translation when they work as translators. They should be able to confront the translated text with the original text, assess earnings and losses and show self-correction capacity. It is this accurate revision of the output that will definitely result in a final translation of higher quality (Gerding-Salas, 2012). The ability to discuss translations presented in an objective way is pivotal to the students' competence in translation. They are able to choose efficient translation strategies that help them cope with long texts or structures.

Students should be exposed to the various translation strategies in the analysis, transfer and restructuring of a text. Students should be trained to decide how they should restructure the same message in a different language in such a way that is common for the readers in that language. In each paragraph, sentence or translation unit, the choice of the translation strategy must be the most useful one for the transfer of ideas. It means adopting the most suitable strategies and techniques to the requirement of the text rather than adopting a certain strategy and using it forever.

According to Duff (1994), idiomatic expressions are notoriously untranslatable and should therefore not be forced into the TL. Instead, one should try any of the translation strategies at their disposal, or drop it altogether. For example, the idiom *"work his boots off"* has nothing to do with the type of shoes referred to as 'boots". This idiom has no Kiswahili equivalent *(nitatoa viatu vyangu)* and would require an interpretive approach so that one ends up with the equivalent of *"I will do whatever it takes"* or *"I will work tirelessly"* (**nitafanya juu chini).**

Nida and Taber (1969) posit that whatever the difficulty in the translation process, strategies used must aim at the essence of the message and faithfulness to the meaning o the SL text being transferred to the TL text. However, it is impossible to have a near perfect translation.

Gerding-Salas (2012) states that one of the greatest virtues of a good translator is "contextualized intuition". That is, the ability to find the nearest common sense interpretation of the "not found" element within the context. In this sub-section, we have demonstrated that translation plays a role in language learning. Teaching translation helps learners communicate into and from a foreign language. It is also a very valuable classroom activity and can be tailored in such a way that it is highly practical, learner-focused and process based.

Conclusion

This chapter has attempted to show that translation is meant for communication beyond the linguistic equivalence. That translation is a highly effective way of drawing learners' attention to the linguistic, semantic and pragmatic features of the TL. The aim of this chapter was to outline and examine the importance of teaching translation. It has emerged that teaching translation provides practical applications besides producing a good translator. It is important in teaching translation, to pick the most appropriate type of translation at any given time. To translate successfully requires a deep knowledge of both source and target culture, in order to ease the transposition of ideas and concepts. It has also emerged that translation, as the process of conveying messages across linguistic and cultural barriers, is an eminently communicative activity, one whose use could well be considered in a wide range of teaching situations than may currently be the case. Knowledge of the process of translation would assist learners analyze the message in the SL text, transfer and restructure it in the TL text, to the level that is most appropriate for the intended audience. Whatever the difficulty in the translation process, procedures must aim at the essence of the message and faithfulness to the meaning of the SL text being transferred to the TL text.

This chapter concludes that translation can be accounted for naturally within the Relevance Theory of Communication, and that the notion of meaning analysis within context is central to this theory. In teaching translation, The Relevance Theory can be used by learners to obtain optimal relevance by paying attention not only to linguistic equation of meaning, but also the paralinguistic implications of the message being conveyed. The theory is important in guiding them to comprehend not only the meaning of words, sentences and discourse structures, but also the symbolic nature of events and the objects that are mentioned in the discourse. In order to remain relevant, learners' translations must be connotatively or denotatively guided depending on the context. Suffice to say that teaching translation helps learners communicate into and from a foreign language. It gives one a chance to see the opportunities of translation, test them through learning and then use them through teaching.

References

Bassnet-McGuire, S. 1980. *Translation studies.* NewYork: Mathue and Co. Ltd.

Biguenet, J and Schulte, R. 1989. *The craft of Translation.* London: University of Chicago Press Ltd.

Carmen, M. 1994. *Approaches to the Teaching of Translation.* Africa Vidal Claramonte: Universidad de Salamanca.

Cartford, J.C. 1965. *A Linguistic Theory of Translation: An essay in Applied Linguistics.* London: Oxford University Press.

Dra, J.E 2010. *Teaching Translation.* Indonesia: Petra Christian University.

Duff, A, 1994. *Translation:*Oup

Gerding-Salas, C. 2012.*Teaching Materials and Techniques for the Communicative Translation Class.* Universitat Leipzid – Universidad de Concepcion.

Gutt, E.A. 1989. *Translation and Relevance.* London: University College London.

Hatim, B. 2001.*Teaching and Researching Translation.* Essex: Pearson Education Ltd.

Hervey, s. and Higgins, I. 1992.*Thinking Translation.* Routledge.

Kussmaul, J. 2008. *Training the Translator.* Newyork: John Benjamins Publishing Co.

Munday, J. 2008. *Introducing Translation Studies: Theories and Applications.* Oxon: Routledge.

Newmark, P. 1995. *A Textbook of Translation.* Library of congress catalogues – in Publication Data.

Nida, A.E.1975. *Language structure and Translation.* Stanford: Stanford University Press.

Nida, E.A. and Taber, C.R. 1969. *The Theory and Practice of Translation.* Leiden:E.J.Brills.

Sperber, D. and Wilson, D. 1986. *Relevance, communication and cognition.* Oxford: Basil Backwell Ltd.

Zhonggang, S. 2006. „*A relevance Theory Perspective on Translating the Implicit Information in Literary Texts.*" A journal of Translation: Volume 2, Number 2.

Chapter Five

Translation in French Language Teaching and Learning

Velma Muyela

Introduction

There has been a steady increase of public secondary schools offering French as a foreign language on the school curriculum. This growth is a direct response to the awareness by the larger Kenyan population that, other foreign languages apart from English, are of necessity becoming increasingly essential in today's economic, political and social global set up. Kenya hosts the headquarters of United Nations and a number of other international agencies, all of which use foreign languages in their day to day operations thus giving an opportunity for employment. Also, there is a notable population from the African Francophone that has made Nairobi a multi-cultural herb. It is also the second most learnt foreign language in Kenya.

Consequently, there is an impetus to promote the learning of the French language as these factors explain the interest for the Kenyan student in learning French as a second language. This article explores the methods of teaching French as a second language and whether these methods do have a direct impact on the number of students that choose or drop the subject at secondary level. The examination of these methods is in order to establish whether the methods create an ideal opportunity for effective foreign language learning in the classroom. The chapter presents a description of the two methods of language learning in secondary schools with a view of drawing useful conclusions on the attributes and success of each of the methods as applies to the Kenyan situation. The author uses library research as well as an overview of personal testimonies from teachers of French.

In the French syllabus tailored for the secondary school level, one of the general objectives is to equip learners with the basic communicative skills for effective communication where French is required. The writer sets out to look at the methods of language learning and how they contribute towards meeting of the set objective in the syllabus.

Learners of foreign languages (French, German and Arabic) are introduced to the new language for the first time in Form One. The foreign language is put under a group of subjects called technical subjects (French, German, Arabic, Music, and Business Studies) where a student takes one subject according to a circular by Kenya National Examination Council on the guidelines for subject selection in secondary schools. In some schools, students choose one of these subjects at the end of form one, while others are exposed to all the subjects in this category and then made to pick one at the end of Form Two. The criterion used to guide this choice is pegged on either performance in class or personal interest in the language by the student or availability of teachers and teaching materials. At this level the teacher is faced with the challenge of the number of students that will proceed with French and sit for the National examinations. As reported in Omusonga's research chapter , many students drop French at the end of Form Two such that "only one student out of three carries on with the subject up to KCSE." His findings further establish that performance of this subject at KCSE examinations is very poor "with 60% of the students failing to get the minimum required grade of C+ to access university education"(Omusonga et al 2009)The interest of this article is to shade light on the methods of teaching French in secondary schools and whether this relates in some way to the low enrolment of students pursuing French up to the end of the secondary education.

What are the methods of Teaching French as a Second Language?

At university level, students training to become French teachers take a course called: Subject Methods- French. This is a course taken in preparation for the Teaching Practice exercise in secondary schools. In this unit, the future teachers of French are exposed to various topics that are to equip them for the teaching of the foreign language, one of which is "French language learning skills: listening, speaking, reading and writing. Methods of teaching: dictation, discussion, comprehension, grammar and vocabulary." Based on this platform, this article focuses on two widely used methods of foreign language learning: the Grammar Translation Method and The Communicative Approach, in order to highlight the merits and challenges that each method has and how this affects the learning of French in Kenyan secondary schools.

The Grammar Translation Method

A method in language learning refers to "a plan for presenting the language material to be learned and keeping upon selected approach". A brief description of the Grammar Translation method shows that this is one of the oldest methods of language learning. It is said to have its roots in the teaching of the Latin and Greek. It is believed "that a method in language teaching determines how much and what is taught... that therefore the method "deals with selection, grading, presentation, and repetition". This method lays emphasis on the teaching of formal grammar along with translation.

Distinguishing Features

The Grammar Translation method focuses on translating grammatical structures, vocabulary, conjugations and general grammar rules to the learners. It is to be noted that a major tenet of this method is to stress to the learner the importance of correct forms rather than basic communication. For example, in a Form one class where the teacher has the major task to interest the learners to this "strange" language, part of the basic formation is to make clear rules governing French grammar.

The learners being introduced to the foreign language for the first time have to for example know that objects are either "she" or "he". The question the teacher has to keep answering at this point is "How do we tell that a door is "she" and a desk is "he" (La Porte/ Le pupitre). The learner is taken through the rigors of verb conjugations: the use of personal pronouns (the regular and the irregular verbs) and verb endings. For instance, in order for them to say: My name is.../ I am a Kenyan (verb *S'Appeler* and *Etre*), - *Je m'appelle.../ Je suis Kenyan*, they need to first learn the rules of conjugation and the rule of personal pronouns;. The use of *'Tu'* – you singular- which is used to address peers and members of the family and the use of *'Vous'* –you - singular / plural which is used to address people in a formal situation. The teacher's focus here is for the learner to be able to conjugate the verbs correctly and then construct the sentences noting the form and proper usage.

Techniques commonly used in the French classroom.

"A technique is practicable; that which actually takes place in a classroom. It is a particular trick, stratagem, or contrivance used to accomplish an immediate objective".

The following techniques have been cited in this article as they have been mentioned in the conversations with this writer by a randomly selected number of secondary school teachers of French:

- **The Deductive Application** of Rule which aims at the learner understanding grammar rules and their exceptions and applying them to new examples. Emphasis is put on the learner paying close attention to these grammar rules and not necessarily on communication in practical situations. This technique does not encourage the students' communicative competence.

- **Fill-in-the-blanks** where the teacher tests the grasp of grammar structures learnt by designing exercises that include filling in gaps in sentences with words or items of a particular grammar feature.

- **Use Words in Sentences** – this technique is done in writing. It helps the learner to practice words learnt in isolation by creating sentences to illustrate they know the meaning and use of new words.
- **Memorization** -the learners memorize vocabulary lists and grammatical rules. This technique may help the learner with the required level of vocabulary at each stage, but does not necessarily lay emphasis on putting this vocabulary to effective communication where French is required especially as concerns oral proficiency in the French language; which is the main objective of learning French at secondary school level.
- **Composition** - the learners are given writing tasks in the target language on specific topics on the general subject areas charted out in the syllabus. The aim is to make the learner to transfer the knowledge of grammar rules into writing. This is because the aspect of reading and writing is a major focus in this approach to language learning.

What are the challenges

Notably, the Grammar translation form of teaching has challenges that the language teacher encounters in the classroom. Oral submissions by a sample of teachers for the purpose of this article support the assertion that "This method makes language learning slow, uninspiring and dull."

Given that students have to make a choice between French and four other subjects in this group at the end of form two – which actually marks the basic introduction to the language acquisition- it is not surprising as observed by Omusonga et al (2009) that "many students drop out of French at this stage, and in some schools, enrolment in the subject in form 3 remains as low as less than 5 students." In this research chapter, Omusonga submits that "In fact, only one student out of three carries on with the subject up to KCSE. Consequently, only 1.5% of the total number of students enrolled in secondary schools in Kenya study French subject." From this observation, this article queries whether there isn't a direct connection between the teaching methods at this basic level, to the learners' luck of interest in the subject by the end of form 2.

As has been noted, "Another problem with this method is that most of the teaching is done through explanation in the learner's first language." The challenge then at this early stage of teaching French to the Kenyan student at secondary level is that their knowledge and fluency in the

English language is more advanced. This therefore creates the task of explaining these rules in English, which brings about a situation for the teacher, as voiced by one of the interviewees, to" teach French in English". This involves translating words, phrases, and sentences from French to English. Due to the need to translate, the lack of a good dictionary (English/French and French/ English), can impair a learner's ability to do the tasks during a learning activity since the work demands high dependency on the dictionary. Where the teacher employs this method at the onset of language learning, elements of oral communication in form of conversation and other relevant strategies are suspended in favour of written work in form of grammar exercises and reading comprehension texts. Consequently, as has been noted with concern, at the end of form Two the students feel discouraged at not being able to understand and express themselves competently at the most basic level of the language. Therefore, the reason for many of them dropping the Language and opting for other optional subjects in that group.

What are the Merits?

The learning of French is not left exclusively to one method. It is an integration of several suitable methods and as such, from a general perspective, it is possible to acknowledge the value of this approach. This method helps the students to master both French and English Grammar since there is much correlation of the two languages during activities in grammar, reading and comprehension. Students are able to learn easily meanings of words through direct translation from English to French, since "the method of comparing and translation of the learned language with the native language provides reference for students."

The Communicative Approach

The communicative language teaching method has risen as a result of the ever growing demand for a better command of the French language at the end of secondary school level. This is stated in one of the objectives of the French curriculum which is to equip learners with basic communicative skills. As much as grammar is crucial to language learning, "Language is no longer seen as being learnt through mechanical exercises, it's developed through students interacting and engaging."(Martin Williams, 2011) The need for good communication skills, coupled with the continued search for relevant and appropriate methods of effective language learning, has forced the French teacher in the Kenyan context to consider an integrated approach over the years. In an article that traces the development of the teaching of French in the last fifty years, the writer ascertains that "The evolution in teaching methods from the Traditional Method right through to the Communicative Approach in the Kenyan situation has always been interspersed with recourse to the Grammar – Translation (Chokah, 2013)" The article further points out that "Communicative Approach arrived with as its main objective, to center the learning process on the learner and enable him to *communicate* in the foreign language." (2013:4)

Communicative Language Learning in the French classroom

What is communicative language learning to the French teacher in the Kenyan situation?

This question is posed because Jack C. Richards raises an Important point that:

Perhaps the majority of language teachers today, when asked to identify the methodology they employ in their classrooms, mention "communicative" as the methodology of choice. However, when pressed to give a detailed account of what they mean by "communicative," explanations vary widely. Does communicative language teaching, or CLT, mean teaching conversation, an absence of grammar in a course, or an emphasis on open-ended discussion activities as the main features of a course?

(Communicative Language Teaching, 2006)

Taking note of how the teacher understands and interprets this methodology is deemed crucial in line with achieving set goals of language learning in a classroom environment; the main goal being "the teaching of communicative competence". According to Richards, competence refers to the *"knowledge we have of a language that accounts for our ability to produce sentences in a language. It refers to knowledge of the building blocks of sentences (e.g., parts of speech, tenses, phrases, clauses, sentence patterns) and how sentences are formed."* (2009: 3).

Therefore, from the general definition to the more specific definition of communicative competence, we can say that for the teacher in the classroom, communicative competence is the ability of the student to use language- at every level of learning- for meaningful communication. This article is then rightly concerned about this core aspect of the communicative approach, which though widely preferred, and consequently more accepted as able to respond to demands of language learning in the modern (global) setting, it begs the question: does it enhance the status of the French language in terms of achieving the set objectives of the syllabus?

Aspects of Communicative Competence and Classroom Activities

School text book writers have responded to the change of the syllabus that accommodates the communicative aspects of language learning. Some of the text books available for the secondary student by Kenya Institute of Education and currently used as teaching material, are: **Parlons Français**, **Entre Copains** and **Au sommet.** The following are some of the activities reflected in these text books: role play, interviews, pair-work, and conversations based on *les documents authentiques*. While these activities have been used effectively allowing the teacher to manipulate learning materials available, the teacher needs to put into consideration aspects of communicative competence one of which is "Knowing how to maintain communication despite having limitations in one's language knowledge (e.g., through using different kinds of communication strategies) "(Richards, 2009:3).

Discussions with fellow colleagues in the classroom show that, usually French teachers in Kenya have the challenge of designing student centered activities that give opportunities to the students to use the language that they are learning. The students, generally, only get to speak the language within the classroom setting where the teacher animates the given oral exercises while encouraging the learners to work in groups or in pairs. Despite this challenge, the communicative approach still provides a motivating environment in the French language class. It is quite rewarding for the students, especially the beginners (form ones) to use picture stimuli such as photographs of a school, a café, a supermarket, a house, class room objects e.t.c to make simple sentences: *c'est une école / je vais à l'école,/ Mon école s'appelle.../ Voila une maison / J'habite dans une maison.* Such authentic documents, as is validated by the learners' response, "support a more creative approach to teaching" since they relate closely to the learners' requirements and expectations, as they experiment with a second language.

Conclusion

The integration of methods and approaches mentioned earlier in this article confirms that no one method is wholesomely equipped for the teaching of French. One has to appreciate that language learning is a gradual process that demands focus on the four language skills: listening, reading speaking and writing for use of language creatively and productively. The low enrolment of learners of the French language in Kenyan secondary schools cannot be pegged solely on the methods and approaches of language learning. While researching for material for this article, the writer noted that in an article titled "***The Expansion of French***

Language Lies in Africa" (Fatunde, 2012), similar concerns were voiced by participants in an international conference of French teachers held in Durban; South Africa. The participants were keen on discussing ways of making French attract more students in an environment that has French competing with other foreign languages.

Therefore in conclusion, it is apt to corroborate with those who have previously researched on this issue. That, there is definitely a gap when one looks at the suggested teaching approaches, the availability of effective teaching/ learning materials and the emphasis of an exam – oriented syllabus. The task of maintaining an upward enrolment of students taking French at Form Three and Form Four level is a serious undertaking that needs to be addressed urgently since the solution lies in a amalgamation of areas such as: teacher training programmes with emphasis on appropriate methods, techniques, and curriculum implementation policies.

Works Cited

Brigid Moira Burke. "Rituals and Beliefs Ingrained in World Language". Academy Publisher. 2011

Chokah, Milcah. "Fifty years of the teaching/learning of French as a foreign language in Kenya: Challenges for teachers and learners. " International Journal of Education and Research Vol. 1 No. 3 March 2013.Print(online)

Chaugule, S."The Communicative Approach to Language Teaching", Articlebase September, 2009.

Fatunde, Tunde."The Expansion of the French Language lies in Africa", University World News, 16th October 2013, Print (online)

Machidah, Sayuki, "Astep forward to using Translation to teach a foreign/second Language". Electronic Journal of FLT, VOL 5, 2008

Omusonga, T . et al. "Matching intended and actual French curriculum objectives in secondary schools in western province ". Educational Research and Review Vol. 4 (6), June 2009,Print

Richards, Jack. Communicating Language Today. New York.: Cambridge University Press, 2006.

Williams, Martin." *Whats the best way to teach languages?*" Journal of Language Teaching and Research, Vol. January 2011

Chapter Six
Interpretation in Judicial Settings
Gatitu Kiguru, Emily A. Ogutu and Martin C. Njoroge
Introduction

This chapter focuses on interpreting in judicial settings and it takes the approach of identifying possible problem areas and suggesting ways of solving these problems. To ground the discussion on court interpreting, the chapter begins with a brief historical view of the development of court interpreting as a profession. This is followed by a discussion of the professional requirements for court interpreting and illustrations, from the Kenyan context, the errors that could arise if high professional standards are not maintained. The chapter ends with suggestions on how to ensure quality interpreting in the courtroom set up.

Translation studies are a branch of comparative linguistics without the synchronic versus diachronic distinctions that characterize most comparative language studies. This is because translation studies are concerned with relationships of meaning between languages and these relationships could be related or unrelated to social factors or the constraints of time and space. The language relationship that is the subject of translation studies is the process through which meaning already expressed in one language is transferred and expressed in another language. A distinction is thus made between the **Source Language** (SL), which is the language *from* which meaning transferred, and the **Target Language** (TL), which is the language *into* which meaning is transferred.

Catford (1) defines translation as 'a process of substituting a text in one language for a text in anther'. However, some scholars use the term translation when the process of substituting meaning involves written texts reserving the term interpreting for a process of text substitution that involves spoken language. This distinction is the basis of the debate on whether interpreting is part of translation studies or a totally independent field. This point will be taken up later.

As Munday (4-5) notes, it is also important to note that the term translation itself can be used in different senses. Translation can refer to the general area of study that concerns itself with the transfer of meaning across languages or the product of this transfer of meaning. Translation or translating can also mean the process of transferring meaning from one language to the other. Translation studies also focus on the different

types of translation. These translation types are a factor of language in that they are categorized on the basis of the different domains and uses language is used for. These domains and uses of language provide thematic areas under which translation studies fall. The following is a list of such thematic areas as suggested by Munday (7).
- History of translation
- Literary translation
- Research models in translation studies
- Gender and translation
- Translation and globalization
- Legal translation
- Translation and training translators

Translation versus Interpreting

The distinction between translation and interpreting is taken by some scholars to be a distinction between parallel fields of study. Munday (13) observes the "Inclusion of interpreting as a sub-category of human translation ... [is] disputed by some scholars". The basis of the dispute is that the requirements for and activities in interpreting are very different from those in translation. Without seeming to dispute or water down the need for such a distinction, we adopt the position interpreting is encompassed in the wider field of translation studies.

Studies on interpreting lead us to the different types of interpreting. On way of classifying the types of interpreting is on the basis of the place where interpreting takes or the subject matter of the discourse being interpreted place. On the basis of this we can have
- Conference interpreting
- Business interpreting
- Medical (doctor – patient) interpreting
- Court interpreting

The last type of interpreting is the focus of the rest of this chapter with the discussion touching on some aspects of interpreter training, criticism of interpretations and policy on interpreting.

Court Interpreting

The practice of court interpreting has a long history. Mikkelson (4) asserts that 'it is safe to assume that the practice of court interpreting is almost as old as the practice of law'. On her part Moeketsi (1995) observes that court interpreting 'dates back to the 17th century when the colonialists first set foot on our shores' (12). The 'shores' Moeketsi refers to are of South Africa but her observation could hold true for the rest of the African countries where modern dispute management systems, of which courts are a part, are part of the colonial legacy. Court interpreting is also taken to be part of legal interpreting. The latter term is all encompassing and refers to interpreting that is done in settings where decisions of a legal nature are to be done and the interpreting is meant to facilitate such decisions. Such settings could include courts, police interrogation rooms, immigration departments' offices, lawyer-client conferences to name a few.

Despite its long history, it is only recently that court interpreting acquired a professional status. The trial of the Nazi war criminals after the end of the 2nd World War is taken by many to be the single event that birthed court interpreting as a profession. Gaiba (33) gives several reasons for this, the major one being the fact that all the victorious war allies were represented at the trials and since they spoke different languages, it became necessary to have interpreter services. In addition, the trials generated huge public and media interest worldwide and consequently it was decided that the proceedings would be conducted using simultaneous interpretation into diverse languages. This was the first time that simultaneous interpreting was being used in the court set up and interpreters had to be trained on the job. Even today, Mikkelson (5) notes, many court interpreters have to learn their skill 'by the seat of their pants.'

However, the years after the Nuremburg trials (as the Nazi war criminal trials held in Nuremburg, Germany came to be known) saw a rise in demand for quality court interpreting services. This led to the initial attempts at training, certification and regulation of court interpreters as a professional group. Mikkelson (11) traces the first regulation of court interpreting to Sweden in the 70s where a state authorization exam for court interpreters was first administered. The U.S.A., Australia, Canada and the United Kingdom followed suit by introducing court interpreter examinations that led to the certification of professional practitioners. In addition to the interpreter examination, the professional status of court interpreters was enhanced by the establishment of professional organizations the first one being the California Court Interpreters Association (CCIA) which was established in 1971 (Mikkelson, 6).

The growth of court interpreting as a profession has not happened uniformly in all countries of the world as some can clearly be said to be a head of the others in this growth. But generally, the driving force behind the development of court interpreting as a profession remains two fold. First, there is increasing awareness 'of the barriers language differences present to the administration of justice' which leads to the need for interpreting (González, Vásquez & Mikkelson 15) and second there is increasing awareness 'of the need to ensure the quality of interpreting services in the judiciary' (Mikkelson 6). The next sections address these twin needs of interpreting services and quality interpreting in the court setup.

The Need for Interpreter Services in Courts

Conflict is part of the human society and; for this reason, societies have developed mechanisms for managing conflict. Modern dispute resolution system through judicial proceedings is one such mechanism. Courts are an arena where parties to a dispute meet before an impartial arbiter and each party gets a chance to present its version of facts and challenge those of the adverse party. On the basis of such presentations and any other evidence adduced before the court, the neutral arbiter is expected to arrive at a judgment that is binding to all the parties. Court proceedings are largely linguistic events, with the direct and cross examination phases of a trial involving questions from the examining party and responses from a witness. Though questions are posed to the witness and the witness' responses directed at the examiner, the participants in courtroom discourse are aware that their utterances are meant for the primary addressee: the presiding judge or magistrate or the jury. Indeed, such contributions constitute the court record that is the basis of ruling and judgments.

Therefore, given the centrality of language in litigation, when the parties to a dispute do not share a common language, or in instances where a litigant does not understand the official language of the court, a potential for a communication breakdown presents. This is the breakdown a court interpreter steps in to prevent. In doing so, the interpreter fulfill a variety of functions: 'They...enable attorneys to communicate with their clients, interpret court proceedings for defendants and litigant, and interpret witness testimony for the court' (Mikkelson 10). She adds that in these roles the interpreter, just like the presiding judge or magistrate, serves as an impartial officer of the court.

Court interpreting is different from other types of interpreting in a number of ways. To start with, it differs from conference interpreting because whereas conference interpreters only interpret from language A into language B, court interpreters are expected to interpret from language A into B then from Language B into A. For instance, in a conference situation where a speaker uses English but a participant only understands Russian, the conference interpreter would only be expected to interpret what is said in English and render it in Russian However, in a scenario where the official language of the court is English and a witness only understands Gikuyu, the interpreter would be expected to render the questions posed in English into Gikuyu and then render the witness responses given in Gikuyu into English. This makes court interpreting to be more demanding.

Moreover in disputing, language use is goal oriented: either to implicate blame or to avoid blame, and the parties to a dispute are legally bound to abide by whatever judgment is rendered. This means that participants in courtroom discourse use a variety of language and pragmatic devices to achieve their divergent goals. In stepping in to facilitate communication, the court interpreter is expected to maintain a very high level of exactitude. The interpreter has to pay attention not just to the words used but also to the nuances behind the words. In addition, the knowledge that the judgment at the end of a trial could mean the deprivation of life or property; incarceration or imposition of fines on one of the parties must also weigh on the interpreter in execution of duty. Furthermore, judicial institutions rely heavily on the goodwill of the public that they serve for the relevance and the continued force of their decisions. As such, the interpreting services offered must contribute to public confidence in judicial institutions.

González, Vásquez and Mikkelson (16) capture the rigorous requirements of court interpreting when they assert:

Instead of a summary, then, the court interpreter is required to interpret the original source material without editing, summarizing, deleting, or adding while conserving the language level, style, tone, and intent of the speaker or to render what may be termed the legal equivalence of the source language. ... Court interpreters are primarily charged with delivering to the court and a non-English speaking defendant linguistic equivalent of all spoken and written communication.

This is such a tall order for the court interpreter and we now look at what is required in order for the interpreter to deliver such high levels of equivalence.

Requirements for the Job
1. Bilingualism

The basic requirement for a court interpreter is to be bilingual. However, as Edwards (1) notes 'Bilingualism does not guarantee the ability to interpret'. At best, bilingualism is an indicator of the gift of interpreting but on its own does not qualify one to be an interpreter. A parallel can be drawn to the fact that whereas most people have two legs and can run, this fact on its own does not qualify them to run in the Olympics. A court interpreter additionally needs to be bicultural because an interpreter mediates not just between languages but also between cultures. Different cultures have idiosyncratic customs and behaviours that are uniquely expressed in their languages, and have no direct equivalents in other cultures and languages or their equivalents could be meaningless in the TL.

Interpreting Skills

Court interpreters need to be proficient in the three major modes of interpreting that are used in the courtroom setting. We look at each one of them in turn below.

a) **Sight Interpreting:** González, Vásquez and Mikkelson (401) define sight interpretation as a hybrid between translation and interpreting as it involves the unrehearsed interpretation of written documents, such as charge sheets, affidavits and expert witness' reports, during a trial. In sight interpreting (abbreviated SI), also known as sight translation, the interpreter is expected to silently read a document written in language A while loudly rendering its contents in language B. This is common in the arraignment phase of a trial and during direct and cross examination phases when written documents in the official language of the court are produced, but a witness or defendant is not conversant with this language.

The challenge in sight interpreting mainly lies in the fact that the interpreter is simultaneously engaged to perform three demanding cognitive activities. The interpreter has to read and understand a chunk of the document, then loudly render the same into the TL while at the same time reading the next chunk and preparing to render it. Moeketsi (120) observes that 'good sight interpreters produce an output so smooth and rhythmic that the audience may be deceived as far as the complexities of the activity is concerned'. It is worth remembering that apart from searching for the right words in which to frame the TL message, the interpreter may as well be searching for correct syntactic ordering of these words in cases where the SL and the TL have different syntactic ordering rules. Moreover, the interpreter still is bound to reflect all the legal and technical terms in the documents into a language that may not have equivalent terms. This makes González, Vásquez and Mikkelson (407) conclude that sight interpreting call not just for linguistic agility but for mental agility as well.

b) **Consecutive Interpreting:** Consecutive interpreting (abbreviated CI) can best be defined with reference conference setting which is where the skill has been perfected. Jones (5) says that in conference interpreting 'the interpreter listens to the totality of a speaker's comments, or at least a significant passage, and then reconstitutes the speech with the help of notes taken while listening.' But Mikkelson (71) notes that this style of consecutive interpreting known as long consecutive cannot work in the courtroom setting where interpreters are duty bound to conserve all elements of the SL message as they render it into the TL. In long consecutive interpreting, conference interpreters edit out aspects of speaker hesitations, self correction and hedges as their goal is to render a polished form in the TL. But such pragmatic aspects are usually of great significance in the courtroom where fact finders focus not on just what a defendant or witness has to say but also on the demeanor of the speaker. As such, court interpreters use the short or sequential style of consecutive interpreting where instead of dealing with entire speeches or large chunks of information, the interpreter consecutively interprets smaller idea units such as clauses or a series of them.

It needs to be noted that in CI, as much as there are two people speaking, their speech, ideally, should not overlap. The interpreter listens as the other party is speaking and when done, the interpreter renders the TL version. This is a major advantage in CI for the interpreter because he or she gets to hear the SL message, at least a part of it, before interpreting it. However CI still has the disadvantage of being time consuming as there is a sense in which twice the time is taken to say one thing. For this reason, CI is nowadays shunned in conference and courtroom settings in which advances in technology allows for simultaneous interpreting.

Apart from being time consuming, CI also has the disadvantage of being very taxing on the short term memory. Court interpreters are not expected to give a summary or the gist of what a speaker says but must render all aspects of the SL message as explained above. Consequently, if a speaker says too much before pausing, there is likelihood that the interpreter could forget some vital bits of the message. The interpreter, therefore, needs to be well versed with some situation control techniques, as will be discussed in the next section. However, in the courtroom setting, it has been observed that when people are aware that their utterances are being interpreted, they pause after an idea unit, mostly a sentence, to allow for interpreting (Kiguru 92).

Perhaps the greatest challenge in CI has little to do with the process of interpreting but the role of the interpreter in the discourse. It needs to be remembered that the interpreter is a facilitator of communication between the key discourse parties in the litigation process. To this end, the interpreter ought to render his or her services as unobtrusively as possible so that it remains clear just who the key participants in the discourse are.

For instance, when a lawyer poses a question to a witness who, in turn answers, the two are the key participants in the exchange plus the fact finder who is the primary addressee. But CI could potentially change these roles. This is because in CI, at some intervals, the key parties are silent and the interpreter takes the center stage in the communication process. This, as De Jongh (7) observes, draws undue attention to the interpreter rather than deflecting it. Thus, there is a greater demand for perfection in rendering the TL message, as mistakes made by the interpreter are more easily detectable.

c) Simultaneous Interpreting: Simultaneous Interpreting (abbreviated SI) is defined as 'the technique whereby the interpreter speaks at the same time as the SL speaker' (González, Vásquez and Mikkelson 359). The technique, whose use in the courtroom setting can be traced to the Nuremburg trials, is by far the most complex as it requires the interpreter to listen and speak at the same time. The interpreter has to listen to the SL speaker, understand a part of what he or she says and begin rendering it in the TL. At the same time, the interpreter is listening to the next utterance and processing it in readiness for rendering it in the TL. Moreover, the interpreter has little control over the pace at which the SL message is given, and also has no idea where the SL message is headed, all these being factors at the control of the speaker (Mikkelson 73).

In judicial proceedings, SI is mainly used to interpret rulings and judgments. This means that the interpretation is from the official language of the court into the language the defendant understands. It needs to be noted that SI cannot be as accurate as CI. SI requires a lot of linguistic and mental juggling which leads Moeketsi (117) to aptly comment 'the simultaneous interpreter is a performer who passes all understanding'.

2. Language Skills

The other job requirement for the court interpreter has to do with language skills and linguistic knowledge. As mentioned in 1.0, interpreters need to be bilingual and have a high competence in the languages they work in. This competence should be in the language skills of listening, note taking and speaking. They should fluently use different registers and styles of each of the languages and have knowledge of slang terms and idiomatic expressions used by different social groups. A good masterly legalese with its unique vocabulary and syntax is also a mandatory requirement for the court interpreter (Hewitt 39).

3. Linguistic Knowledge

In addition, apart from just knowing the languages they work in, interpreters should also know about these languages. This is to say that a basic linguistic knowledge is necessary for a court interpreter. Such knowledge would include word formation processes, morphological typologies, syntactic rules and a basic knowledge of translation theory. Such knowledge is necessary especially in cases where the interpreter has to work in languages with different morphology and syntactic rules. In such cases, linguistic knowledge would be an important assent in problem predicting and solving. Specifically, interpreters need to know the challenges in interlingual and intercultural communication. We highlight a few such challenges below as identified by González, Vásquez and Mikkelson (306-10).

a) **Different Semantic Areas** – this means that SL and TL words that are equivalents do not belong to the same semantic areas. For example the English word 'house' can be taken to be equivalent to the Gĩkũyũ word 'nyũmba'. In English 'house' can denote multiple meanings such as (i) dwelling place, (ii) parliament (iii) an old and famous family (iv) people living in a house (v) a company involved in a particular kind of business. The Gĩkũyũ term 'nyũmba' does not denote meanings (ii) and (v) but it denotes meaning (i) and can also be said to denote meanings (iii) and (iv). However, the Gĩkũyũ meanings of 'house' that have reference to people are different from those in English. Any family, not necessarily an old or famous one, can be called 'nyũmba' and the term is also used in an extended way to refer to the whole Gĩkũyũ tribe as in 'nyũmba ya Gĩkũyũ na Mũmbi' meaning 'the house of Gĩkũyũ and Mũmbi' (these two being the mythical founders of the tribe). In the English expression 'don't wake up the whole house' the word 'house' refers to people living in a house but they need not be related, and thus the expression could well serve in a dorm house. In Gĩkũyũ, the term 'nyũmba' is mainly used where the speaker wants to emphasize a family relationship and thus excludes people who are not of a said family. So, it would be more correct to interpret the term 'house' in 'don't wake up the whole house' as 'andũ' (people) in Gĩkũyũ so that we have 'don't wake up all the people'. The point is as much as 'house' and 'nyũmba' are equivalents and have some meanings that overlap, these meanings may not all be in the same semantic areas and there are times when the choice of 'nyũmba' for 'house' and vice versa may miss out on some subtle distinctions.

b) **Mismatched Levels of Precision between the SL and TL** – in expressing concepts, languages do not always have the same degrees of specificity. A term in the SL language may be inherently precise in a way its equivalent in the TL is not. For example, the English term 'guilt' as used during the reading of the charges 'Are you guilty or not guilty' is distinct from the concept of 'truth'. In law, it could be true that somebody received some money but it is successfully argued that he or she is not guilty of receiving a bribe given that the term 'guilty' has in it elements of responsibility necessarily with respect to a crime. But this term is substituted with 'true' when rendered in Kiswahili so that a defendant is asked to respond to 'Ni kweli au si kweli' (is it true or not true) during the reading of the charges. Kiswahili may not have a term that is as precise in meaning and connotation as the English term 'guilty'.

Also, the word 'hear' in English is specific to the auditory sense, but in Gĩkũyũ, the equivalent 'kũigua' (to hear) can apply to many of the senses. Thus it would be the equivalent to the English words 'hear' (hear noise), 'feel' (feel cold), 'feel' (feel pain) and can even apply to the olfactory sense and the sense of taste.

Another example is the verb 'tease' which in English allows for the person doing it to either be joking or intending to embarrass or hurt another person. Thus, 'They were teasing him' could be taken to show malicious intent or just people being jocular. If the term 'tease' is translated into Gĩkũyũ, a choice would have to be made on the intent behind the teasing. This will lead to 'kũmũthakĩra' (to play with him) if the intent is taken to be jocular or 'kũmũthirĩkia' (to tease so as to embarrass or make angry) if the intent is taken to be malicious.

c) Idiomatic Expressions and Sayings – idioms and sayings are a feature of all languages. The challenge in interpreting such lies in the fact that the words that constitute them function as a unit to express a complete meaning known by the speakers of the language. The meaning expressed is thus not a factor of the words that constitute an idiom or saying. Thus in saying 'It is raining cats and dogs' a speaker is not saying anything about cats or dogs but rather using an expression that conveys the intensity of the rain. Another example from English is the use of an expression like 'I do not think much of him' which is a disparaging remark on the 'him' of the sentence. This can be translated into Kiswahili literally as 'Simfikirii sana' (I don't think a lot / much about him) and it losses any disparaging effect on the 'him'. To retain the disparaging meaning, the utterance would have to be rendered like 'Ninamdharau' (I despise him).

Ethical and Professional Requirements

In discharging their mandate, court interpreters are expected to demonstrate a high level of professional responsibility. This responsibility includes:

a) Upholding Confidentiality – court interpreters may work in an environment in which they become privy to information that is personal or that is privileged and is just meant for the two parties communicating. Interpreters should never share such information with third parties.

b) Impartiality – court interpreters work in environments in which disputes are processed and must always keep in mind that they are officers of the court whose allegiance is to justice and their service is to the public. They must, therefore, avoid any forms of favoritism to any of the parties in a dispute, which could include other officers of the court such as prosecutors and defence counsel.

c) Accuracy and Completeness – in rendering the SL utterances into the TL, court interpreters must always endeavor to conserve all elements of the original utterance. As such, interpreters should not undertake to correct mistakes in the original utterances, raise the levels of formality or edit out vulgarities or obscenities in the SL utterance. In this regard González, Vásquez and Mikkelson (478) categorically assert that 'No matter how incorrect, illogical, incriminating, or non-responsive the statement, the interpreter must translate it unquestioningly, exactly as it was stated'. In other words, judgment of what is correct, sensible, proper, relevant or admissible before the court is outside the mandate of the interpreter.

d) Professional Demeanor – the court interpreter should not show personal emotions like sympathy, like or dislike to either of the parties in a dispute or the subject matter that is the focus of the discourse he or she is interpreting. In addition, the interpreter should strive to remain unobtrusive in the course of duty. However, the interpreter should not fail to correct their own mistakes or point out sources of difficulty such as a witness speaking inaudibly.

The knowledge and skills as well as the ethical considerations discussed above are a summary of what is expected of a professional court interpreter. However, in reality, the belief that bilingualism equals the ability to interpret is still a persistent one. We now focus on court interpreting in Kenyan court, which is done by persons who are bilingual but have no formal training in interpreting or specialized knowledge in linguistics. Our focus is on interpreter errors which we argue could be minimized through training.

Aspects of Interpreter Errors in Kenyan Courts

This section reports on the findings of a study that sought to identify categories of interpreter errors occurring in sampled courts in Kenya. The study sample was drawn from two Chief Magistrates Courts in Nairobi and Thika. A Chief Magistrates administers over a cluster of courts each with a presiding magistrate. Thus, the study collected data from several court presided over by different magistrates and each served by a court clerk. The data were audio recordings of court proceedings that involved interpretation form and into English, Kiswahili and Gĩkũyũ. At the time of the study, English was the sole official language in Kenya, making it the official language of the court.

The study identified grammatical errors and errors of distortion / intrusion to be the most frequently occurring at 20% each of the 65 five interpreter errors identified. These were followed by lexical errors and errors of omission each with a percentage frequency of 17% and 16% respectively. Errors arising from undefined role and ethics had a frequency of 13%. The other errors identified included added information, ambiguity, literal translation and errors arising from the work environment and each had a percentage frequency of less than ten percent. We define and illustrate a few of these errors below. In the examples cited what constitutes an error is in bold type face while interpretations by the researcher are in italics.

Omission

This involves "omitting words, phrases, clauses, ideas, sentences or portions of discourse" in the interpreted utterance (González, Vásquez & Mikkelson 288). When information is omitted, the party for whom the interpretation was meant does not get to hear it. This can lead to anxiety, misunderstanding or the exclusion of one of the parties in a trial.

Of particular note was the observation that interpreters in the study sample were found to regard lengthy discussions between presiding magistrates and prosecutors as 'off-the-record' remarks and thus never interpreted them, even when they were uttered in the presence of litigants and touched on the matter before the court. This practice goes against the ultimate goal of the court interpreting, which is to place the litigant who does not speak the official language of the court in the same position as the one who does. The exchange below illustrates this.

Example 1

Magistrate: Prosecutor, do you realize you have a serious problem here?

Prosecutor: Your Honour?

Magistrate: Why do you people do things this way? Eeh? Tell me, how are you going to connect accused one ... no accused two and three to the robbery? How?

Prosecutor: You Honour, may be if we call the next witness, she ...

Magistrate: No, no no. she is an employee at the bar, and she will only tell us what they found the next morning. Was she there during the robbery?

Prosecutor:	No. she doesn't stay ...
Magistrate:	Even, your first witness, the complainant has said no body was in the premises at that time. Now, look, the stolen items were recovered at the house of the first accused, the 2nd and 3rd accused do not stay in that house. In fact, according to the complainant they were arrested at their homes that are far away from that of the first accused. So how will you connect them to the recovered items?
Prosecutor:	According to the complainant, the 1st accused is the one who told the police that the second accused, who is her brother, brought the items to her house at night together with the third accused. She is the one who showed the police ...
Magistrate:	Is she your witness? Will you call her?
Prosecutor:	Your Honour...
Magistrate:	You see, she is jointly charged with them for the robbery, so she won't testify. You will need may be... do you have a forensics witness, were they called to take finger prints at the bar?
Prosecutor:	No your Honour.
Magistrate:	You see. Do you see the problem you will face? You went ahead and decided to charge them all together. In fact, the only person you can get here is the first accused on the alternative charge of being found in possession of stolen property. I don't see how you will connect the others to the robbery. How did the complainant know that the items were at the house of the first accused?
Prosecutor:	She told the police that somebody told her, but she refused to give the name.
Magistrate:	You see, you are left without a crucial witness. Well, let's proceed, who are you calling now?

Given that none of the discussion in bold typeface is interpreted for the accused person, the concepts of 'presence' and 'due process' are brought into question. Due process demands, among other things, that an accused person be present at every stage. In the incident exemplified above, it could be argued that the three accused persons, who clearly did not understand English, since any utterance from the magistrate or the prosecutor had to be interpreted for them in Gĩkũyũ, are linguistically absent from their own trial, given that matters touching on the case against them are being discussed in open court and they are not privy to the discussion. Justice Lockwood, cited in González, Vásquez and Mikkelson, (49) in a ruling states that such a situation is comparable to one in which a defendant is forced to observe the proceedings from a sound proof booth or seated out of hearing at the rear of the courtroom, being able to observe but not comprehend the criminal processes, whereby the state has put his freedom in jeopardy. Although the exchange above was not directed at the accused persons, they should get to hear and understand because it as a discussion of their case, carried out in open court and in their presence.

But having said that, we must acknowledge that the example above represents what Frishberg, cited in González, Vásquez and Mikkelson (500) calls 'the classic dilemma for the interpreter,'. In the exchange, the magistrate, who should play the role of a neutral arbiter, seems to be pointing out to the prosecutor the weaknesses in his manner of prosecuting the case against the trio. The presiding magistrate explains to the prosecutor the 'serious problem' he will face connecting the 2nd and 3rd accused persons to the crime of robbery. While it could be argued it is unethical for the interpreter not to interpret this exchange, it could also be argued that it would be extremely awkward for the interpreter to render what her boss clearly means to be for the ears of the prosecutor and not of the accused person. The error of omission in such an instance, thus, is not solely of the interpreter's making but also contributed to by the other officers of the court who seem not to appreciate the role of an interpreter in court proceedings.

Distortion and Intrusion

Another problem arising from lack of understanding of the interpreter's role are errors that change or in some way alter the overall or partial meaning of the original message (González, Vásquez & Mikkelson 493-99). The ultimate goal of the interpreter is to conserve every idea and paralinguistic feature in the source message whether or not these ideas seem consequential or appropriate to the formal court setting. But it was observed in the data that interpreters tended distort witness testimony meant for the court record. The likely consequence of this, as the following example shows, is that the court record captures things that were not really part of witness testimony.

Example 2

Witness: Agītwīra omūndū **arute** ngiri īgīrī **nīegūtuoithia** '*college*'

*She told us each of us **to give** Kshs. 2000 **she would make us be selected** to join college.*

Interpreter: She told us **to give her** two thousand shillings each and **she would take us** to college.

The errors shown in bold above are distortion arising from grammar. The example above is from a case where the accused person is said to have acquired money fraudulently. The current witness uses a passive construction in which she does not name the agent that was to receive the said Ksh. 2000 or the one who would make them be selected to join college. But in rendering it, the interpreter uses the active voice and explicitly provides the accused person as the agent receiving the money, and the one responsible for taking the witness to college. Thus the interpreter's rendering makes the witness sound like she categorically placed the accused in a position of blame while in actual fact the witness has not. It needs to be remembered that the court interpreter is the 'voice' of witnesses and accused persons who are unable to express themselves in the language of the court, because the interpretation of the testimony of such persons 'is the only permanent record of what that person said under oath' (González, Vásquez & Mikkelson 485).

Errors Arising from Undefined Role, Procedure and Ethics

Some interpreter errors stem from a general lack of professionalism and a misunderstanding of the role of the interpreter by themselves, the public and even persons working within the court system (González, Vásquez & Mikkelson 209). From the study, it emerged that court interpreters in Kenya work without a clear definition of their duties or clarification of their role in the administration of justice. It is widely held that a court interpreter should strive to be an objective medium through which information is transferred from one language to another. González, Vásquez and Mikkelson (475-513), however, note that some interpreters demonstrate a lack of professionalism by, inter alia, speaking to witnesses in an inappropriate tone, or commanding witnesses to answer questions. Consider the following example.

Example 3

Interpreter: Rīu nīkīī kīūru nainyuī. Kaī mūtaramenya gūkū nī igoti-inī tigwa cibū kūrīa mūikanagīria ciugo ūria mūkwenda? We ūrie ciūria na woria ūgeterera ūcokerio. Nawe ūkahe kahinda to kwanjia kwaria, nīmwaigua?

Language and Translation

Now, what is wrong with you? Don't you realize this is in court and not at the chief's office where you throw words at each other the way you like? *You, you ask questions and after asking you wait to be given an answer. And you, you give me time don't just start talking. Do you hear me?*

The example above is from a cross examination of a witness by an unrepresented accused person. The interpreter betrays his irritation at the way the accused person and the witness are 'throw[ing] words at each other' without giving time for interpretation. The attempt at controlling the verbal output of the two parties sounds more like a not too polite reprimand. By resorting to reprimanding the participants, the interpreter betrays his feelings and opinions about the accused person. González, Vásquez and Mikkelson (498) categorically state that 'interpreters should keep their emotions in check', since an expression of feeling or personal opinion is likely to have an impact on the triers of fact and, as a result, erode the interpreter's impartiality.

Grammatical Errors

The study on which this section reports indentified a variety of grammatical errors which included errors in number, tense and aspect as well as errors in the substitution of active voice for passive voice and substitution of question types. We illustrate the last type of these grammatical errors.

Example 4

Counsel: That cow was sold to you by **the accused person or by his son**?

Interpreter: Ng'ombe īyo wendeirio nī ūyū ūthitangītwo, **naithītiguo**?

*That cow was sold to you by the accused person, **isn't that so**?*

Should be: Ng'ombe īyo wendeirio niūria ūthitangītwo kana nī mūriū?

That cow was sold to you by the person who has been sued or by his son?

The question by the counsel in cross examination is an alternative question where the addressee is meant to choose between 'the accused person' or 'his son'. In rendering it into Gīkūyū, the interpreter the interpreter makes two changes. In the first place, he removes the choices in the original question and just focuses on the accused person, and secondly, he adds a tag to the question which demands the witness confirm the proposition in the question that it is the accused person who sold the cow to the witness.

In courtroom discourse, the use of questions is strategic and thus the choice of question form for examiners is usually carefully thought out. Questions can be arranged in a scale that shows their degree of coerciveness i.e. the extent to which they constrain the response they elicit in terms of form and content. According to Tkačuková (43), the least coercive questions are Wh- questions while the most coercive are tag questions. Seen in this light, the change of question by the interpreter in the example above could have an impact on witness response which may not have been intended by the counsel as cross examiner.

Problem Solving

The preceding section has highlighted interpreter errors that could arise due to poor interpreting. In the judicial setting, the impact of such errors could be big and have many ripple effects. Errors could lead to entry of the wrong information in the court record and this could lead to an erroneous judgment. Such judgments, either singly or incrementally, can have an adverse effect on public opinion on the justice system and or the judicial officers.

We propose that such problems can be mitigated against on two level. The first is through the designing and implementation of a court interpreter training programme and the second is through the formulation policy guidelines on the practice of court interpreting. We will look at each of these problem solving techniques in turn as we suggest what each could entail.

Formal Training for Court Interpreters

The practice of court interpreting has not gained professional status in all countries of the world especially those on the African continent. *Black's Law Dictionary* defines the term profession, with reference to an occupation, practice or vocation, as 'the ability of a person to offer professional services due to the education qualification and expertise in a field'. The mention of educational qualification, in this definition, suggests that the skills required in a profession are mostly mental as opposed to manual. This means that if court interpreting is to be a profession, the practitioners need to undergo some formal training to impart them with requisite knowledge and skills which then need to be developed and sharpened as the interpreter engages in real jobs. The following are some of the skill and knowledge areas that a curriculum on court interpreter training course needs to focus on.

Language Skills

An interpreter by profession is first a student of language. As mentioned in 6.0, an interpreter needs to be well grounded in the languages he or she works in. Edwards (3-4) suggests that an interpreter should have completed a language course before embarking on an interpreter course. This would mean that, though the interpreter course would focus on language, the aim would be to build on such skills and link them to interpreting rather than the focus on starting the teaching of language skills from scratch. The implication here is that to qualify for a court interpreting course, one should have passed well in languages at high school level or one could have a diploma or a degree in language and linguistics. Such prerequisite requirements could at least show that one has an aptitude for interpreting.

The language skills that the interpreting course will seek to strengthen and build on are varied. We present a few below drawing the link they have with the interpreter skills required for the job as discussed in 6.0.

a) ***Oral Language Skills*** – these are perhaps the most utilized by the interpreter in the course of duty. The interpreter needs training on proper articulation of sounds and words as well as the public speaking skills of voice projection, pacing and clear enunciation. These are skills that are necessary in all the three modes of interpreting namely sight interpreting, consecutive interpreting and simultaneous interpreting.

b) ***Reading and Comprehension Skills*** – though different, we group these two skills together as a pointer to the fact that interpreters use all of them concurrently in sight interpreting. In reading, the interpreter should be adept at identifying the main parts of a sentence such as the subject and the verb and distinguish between main and dependent clauses. In addition, the ability to chunk a text into idea units is important as well as the ability to predict the succeeding information by appealing to both knowledge about language and general knowledge. Exercises on paraphrasing, shortening and expanding a text would help in developing comprehension and retention ability which is key in sight interpreting. The reading and comprehension training could also include register manipulation exercises.

c) ***Note Taking Skills*** – Note taking is also a crucial skill especially in consecutive interpreting where the interpreter needs an aid to help him or her retain all aspects of the SL message for rendering when a speaker pauses. Here, court interpreters need to be versed with what is referred to as the Rozan Method. This is a note taking system developed by Jean-François Rozan in 1956 in which the SL message is captured in symbols and a variety of other notations which assist the interpreter to recall the totality of the message. Ultimately, court interpreters are expected to develop a masterly of the system and even come up with their own symbols for representing ideas and other meanings in the SL message which then become aids as the message is rendered into the TL.

Interlingual and Intercultural Interpreting Strategies – these are job specific skills that could help court interpreters deal with potential problems that dog communication across languages and cultures:

a) ***Transposition:*** in rendering the TL message the court interpreter makes changes with regards to parts of speech or word order so that the message conforms to the grammatical rules operating in the TL. For instance, in interpreting 'The money was hers' into Gīkūyū, one has to take note of the use of the definite article 'the' and the feminine gender marking on the pronoun as they are grammatical notions that Gīkūyū does not have. The definiteness of the money can be captured by using the pronoun 'that' while the pronoun would have to be replaced with an appropriate noun. One could have 'Mbeca icio ciarī cia mūtumia / mūirītu ūcio' (money that was of woman / girl that) 'That money belonged to that woman / girl.' In this case the TL message involves the substitution of the article and the pronoun with a pronoun and noun respectively and this is followed by a rearrangement of the word order so that the TL message is meaningful.

At times, the transposition is more drastic depending on the distance between the languages involved. For example, the English sentence 'John had promised me that he would pay Ben the money' would require more drastic transposition when rendered into Gīkūyū because of the verb 'promise'. In the English utterance, the promise is to the speaker but it is made in reference to money to be paid to a third party. In Gīkūyū, the verb equivalent to 'promise' is 'kwīrīra' (to promise) cannot be used by a first person to refer to a promise made to him or her regarding yet another person. So rendering in the sentence above into Gīkūyū, the promise would have to be made to the person the money is to be paid. 'Joni nīanjīrīte atī nīakarīha Beni mbeca icio' (John had told me that he would pay Ben the money). The challenge here is where the verbs 'to promise' and 'to tell' are synonymous, and clearly they are not. One way the interpreter could deal with this is to resort to an intensifier to show the 'telling' was in earnest and this could show it was meant as a promise. 'Joni nīanjīrīte nama atī nīakarīha Beni mbeca icio' (John had told me truthfully that he would pay Ben the money)

b) ***Adaptation:*** this strategy comes in to help deal with cultural differences rather than grammatical ones. Thus, faced with an idiomatic expression or a saying, the interpreter looks for how the TL (and hence culture) expresses the same phenomenon idiomatically. For instance an English speaker could say 'I could not tell them apart. They are like two peas in a pod.' In Kiswahili, the idiom could be '...wanafanana kama mapacha' (they resemble each other like twins). This would be more natural rather than to literally translate the metaphor and demand for more processing effort to the target audience as the metaphor it is not there in Kiswahili.

c) **Amplification:** here the interpreter expands the TL rendering in order to make meaningful a SL term that may not have a simple TL equivalent. 'The money was meant for <u>miscellaneous expense</u>' rendered into Gĩkũyũ would be something like 'Mbeca icio ciarĩ cia <u>mahũthĩro mangĩ ma mwanya</u> / <u>mahũthĩro ma haha na haria</u>' (the money was for <u>other expenses on the side</u> / <u>expenses of here and there</u>) as the language does not have a single word that can be said to the equivalent of 'miscellaneous'.

d) **Explication:** at times, the SL message might mean something implicitly but the same meaning is not explicitly stated. In such a situation, the court interpreter is expected to make such meaning explicit in the TL. For example, the English word 'deceased' is formally used to refer to a dead person. In Gĩkũyũ, there are several potential equivalents but two of them contain implicit information. The terms 'mutigairĩ' and 'mwendwoniirĩ' refer to a deceased person but the former implicitly means that the dead person was married and had children while the latter term implicitly means the dead person was not married and did not have children. Such distinctions could be of significance in succession cases and the interpreter would have to explicitly state the deceased had dependants or not depending on the Gĩkũyũ term used.

In addition to these strategies that smooth out interlingual and intercultural communication, the court interpreter needs to be well versed in general interpreting skill like chunking and décalage. Moeketsi (115) explains chunking to be the skill in which the court interpreter segments the SL message into chunks during simultaneous interpreting. The chunks are usually syntactic or semantic units which an interpreter processes separately. So in interpreting, the interpreter listens and chunks the input SL message. Processes the first chunk by coming up with equivalent semantic and syntactic forms in the TL semantic and renders them. This is done as the interpreter listens to and processes the subsequent chunks in the SL message. Thus, the SL message is managed by dividing it into manageable chunks that allow for processing, rendering and listening to occur simultaneously.

Décalage is a technique that also finds use in simultaneous interpreting. In SI two people are speaking at the same time but the interpreter has to lag behind the speaker so that he or she has content to interpret. The lagging behind of the speaker is what is known as décalage. Knowing how to do this properly is a very crucial skill because the interpreter does not know where the SL message is going. Following the speaker too closely, for example word for word, would obviously lead to a meaningless TL rendering and lagging too far behind would result in the interpreter being overwhelmed by the SL output, processing, rendering and listening. Déclage is thus a delicate balancing act on the part of the court interpreter that would require intensive training through mock exercises involving a variety in pace and register in the SL message as these are the major determining factors as to just how far behind the SL speaker the court interpreter should lag.

Policy Guidelines for Court Interpreting

Without seeming to suggest the value of policy guidelines decreases with time, we wish to assert that such guidelines are most critical for emerging professions. The 9th edition of *Black's Law Dictionary* defines policy as 'the general principles by which a government is guided in its management of public policy.' Policy guidelines for court interpreting emanate from the judicial arm of governments and are meant to oversee the actualization of requirement in many constitutions about the provision of interpreting services for litigants not conversant with the official language of the court or the language of other key participants in judicial proceedings.

The drafting of policy guidelines is an issue that should involve reaching out to various parties that are involved in the administration of justice as well as other parties who have technical knowhow about different aspects of the subject of the policy. Given this, we cannot assume the role of policy makers but, guided by best practice from elsewhere, we will suggest the areas that could be the focus of policy guidelines.

To begin with, it needs to be clear just who needs and qualifies for interpreter services in the courtroom setting. The obvious response would be any litigant who is not conversant with the language of the court. But the issue is more complex because it is necessary to state how competence in a language will be measured. Kiguru (57) reports on presiding magistrates insisting defendants or witnesses use Kiswahili because it is believed that almost everyone in Kenya speaks the language. But if one feels they need to argue their case, whose outcome has far reaching effects on them, in their mother tongue as it is the one they feel more competent in, should one insist they use Kiswahili assuming they can speak it? How we use the languages we speak seems to be the issue rather than just how many languages we speak. But there is the reverse side to this issue. Could litigants take advantage and insist on using a particular language even though they understand and express themselves in the official language of the court with ulterior motives? This would mean that litigants could take advantage of the provision of interpreting services so that they get to hear the message twice (in one of the official languages and then in their mother tongue) so that they end up having a longer time to reflect on questions before they have to respond. This could make the litigation process unnecessarily longer.

The second issue that needs clarification is the role of the interpreter in the justice process. Policy guidelines need to make clear whose interests the interpreter serves. Is it those of the process or the parties in the process. For instance, one of the ways suggested above for dealing with interlingual and intercultural communication challenges is adaptation. Whereas this can work non-controversially when dealing with idioms, should interpreters use this strategy when faced with SL technical vocabulary that have no equivalents in the TL. Should the interpreter assume the adaptation role where he or she tries to simplify and outline court procedures and explain individual questions or should the interpreter take the conservation role where he or she tries to attain equivalence between SL and TL messages and leaves other challenges unresolved? Answering this question is not essay as there is need to look at loop hole that may arise when we adopt either. If interpreters can explain questions and other court procedures, who is to tell how far such explanations can go? If interpreters do not give such explanations and this leads to misunderstandings, is the failure the interpreter's or is it a failure of the wider system?

Thirdly, policy guidelines need to address the related issue of the duties of a court interpreter. This is important because part of being a professional is specialization. Kiguru (99) established that in Kenya, interpreting in courts is done by persons whose official title is Court Clerk. As such, whereas they interpret, they are also expected to, at times concurrently, perform clerical duties such as organizing files, calling out the names of defendants, writing down exhibits produced in court, writing out warrants for the magistrates' signature and providing stationery for the presiding magistrate. This could impact negatively on the interpreting activity which has already been shown to be a very intensive mental activity.

Finally, there is need for policy guidelines on the ethical standards expected of court interpreters in performance of duty. The aspects of confidentiality, impartiality, accuracy and professional demeanor, as discussed in 6.0, need to be made explicit and binding to the practitioners of the profession. Such guidelines would provide for uniformity in the performance of duty by court interpreters as well as provide benchmarks against which quality can be guaranteed.

Conclusion

The need for quality interpreting in the judicial setting cannot be emphasized as the impact of language use in this setting has wide reaching consequences not just for individual litigants but also for judicial institutions. This chapter has given a brief sketch on the historical foundations of court interpreting as a profession and highlighted possible interpreter errors that can occur. In the current world, service providers both in the private and public sectors strive for best practice as the only way of remaining relevant. We urge the same for judicial institutions with regard to interpreter services. There is need to learn from countries that have fully embraced and planned for the growth of court interpreting as a profession. The long term benefits of having professional court interpreters, we assert, far outweigh the short term cost.

Works Cited

Catford, J. C. *A Linguistic Theory of Translation.* Oxford: Oxford UP, 1965. Print.

De Jongh, Elena M. *An Introduction to Court Interpreting: Theory and Practice.* New York: University Press of America, 1992. Print.

Edwards, Alicia B. *The Practice of Court Interpreting.* Philadelphia: John Benjamins, 1995. Print.

Gaiba, Francesca. *The Origins of Simultaneous Interpretation: The Nuremberg Trial.* Ottawa: University of Ottawa P. 1998. Print.

González, Roseann Dueñas, Victoria F. Vásquez and Holly Mikkelson. *Fundamentals of Court Interpretation: Theory Policy and Practice.* Durham: Carolina Academic Press, 1991. Print.

Hewitt, William E. (1995). *Court Interpretation: Model Guides for Policy and Practice in State Courts.* Williamsburg: National Centre for State Courts, 1995. Print.

Holmes, James S. *Translated: Chapters on Literary Translation and Translation Studies.* Amsterdam: Rodopi. 1988. Print.

Jones, Roderick. *Conference Interpreting Explained.* Manchester: St. Jerome, 1998. Print.

Kiguru, Gatitu. "Strategies Employed by Court Interpreters and Aspects of Interpreter Error in Selected Kenyan Courts." Diss. Kenyatta University, 2008. Print.

Mikkelson, Holly. *Introduction to Court Interpreting.* Manchester: St. Jerome, 2000. Print.

Moeketsi, Rosemary. *Discourse in a Multilingual and Multicultural Courtroom: A Court Interpreter's Guide.* Pretoria: Van Schaik, 1999. Print

Moeketsi, Rosemary. (1999). "Redefining the Role of the South African Court Interpreter". *Proteus: Newsletter of the National Association of Judiciary Interpreters and Translators.*8.3-4 (1999). Web.

Munday, Jeremy. *Introducing Translation Studies: Theories and Applications.* London: Routledge, 2001. Print.

Tkačuková, Tatiana. "Lay People as Cross-Examiners: A Linguistic Analysis of the Liberal Case McDonald's Corporation v. Helen Steel and David Morris". Diss. Marsaryk University, Brno. 2010. Web.

Chapter Seven

Translation in a Globalized World

Catherine Waithera Ndung'u

Introduction

Hatim and Munday (2005) define translation as the process of turning an original or "source" text into a text in another language. Translation has mainly been exercised by Christian missionaries who have over time translated the Bible from one language to the other. This has been motivated by the urge to spread the gospel to all parts of the world. Technology has turned the world into a global village which necessitates wider translation to enable easy communication. Globalization has been variously defined but in the context of this chapter, it refers to all those processes by which the peoples of the world are incorporated into a single world society, global society (Beer kens, 2006). Newmark (2003) further defined globalization as the process enabling financial and investment markets to operate internationally, largely as a result of deregulation and continuously improved and intensified communication.

Communication is one of those processes that is vital for the global society to carry out their businesses. Hatim & Munday (2006) identifies three types of translation. Intralingua translation which is translation within the same language, which can involve rewording or paraphrase; interlingual translation which is translation from one language to another, and intersemiotic translation which is translation of the verbal sign by a non-verbal sign, for example music or image. This chapter will deal with the second type of translation, from one language to another. It will delve into translation in a globalized world as it relates to media, communication, culture and conflict.

It is also important to introduce media and communication as they are important aspects of translation in a globalized world. They will feature prominently throughout the discussion of this chapter. The world dictionary defines media as means of communication that reach large numbers of people, such as television, newschapters and radio. Journalists roam around the world seeking for juicy news to feed their insatiable audience through all available channels.

Translation in a globalized world brings on board so many issues. This is because a translation should be similar to the source text as much as possible. Newmark (2003) notes that albeit possible, the success of a translation to successfully make a full restatement of meaning is usually only approximate. This requires the translator to possess important skills of translation. This section describes issues in translation in a globalized world.

Culture

Culture is the characteristics of a particular group of people, defined by everything from language, religion, cuisine, social habits, music and arts (Zimmerman, 2012). Language and culture are closely intertwined as culture is transmitted through language. It is therefore essential to consider the two in the process of translation. The world gives a variety of languages with different cultures (Hymes, 2000) causing translation gain two facets. One facet is being an effective factor in communicating, exchanging cultures and knowledge (IPEDR, 2012). The other facet is making translation difficult. Culture unearths obstacles when translating languages of the world. These obstacles include; religion, culture and limitation and censor.

Religion can be understood only by its cultural language and to translate this religious context we are faced by translation limitations. Religion and culture are intertwined and religion has taken its root from human mind and soul, people accept them by the core of their hearts (Wilson, 2009). Hence, it is difficult to change or distort their beliefs.

Looking at culture, we find that that there arise serious problems for translators that produce far reaching misunderstandings among readers. Transferring cultural information from the source text into the target text poses a lot problems. Venuti, (2002) states that each society or group of people based on their historical background, local situations, and religion with their specific language, construct their own culture which is respected, performed and accepted along with its limitations. Behaviors which are acceptable will vary from location to location. The major problem in translation is influenced by different cultural norms in the source language and target language (Byram, 1989). The translator's responsibility is to choose the norms that take priority over others. It depends on translator's decision whether the cultural norms of the source language, target language, or a combination of both are essential to be considered.

Usually, there is something which is lost during the translation process. Limitation and censor are obstacles that limit translators in conveying the "semantic" message in the receptor language (Venetia, 1994). The other limiting factor which translators encounter is moral filtering being based on religion, family, society rules, and culture, etc. There is also limitation related to different kinds of audiences.

Under this issue of culture in a globalized world, journalists are limited to report and communicate effectively to all their audiences due to the handicap presented by culture. However, there is a positive facet regarding culture and translation. Media in particular is responsible for this fact, that is to communicate culture. Some aspects of communicating culture include; universalizing culture, familiarizing pop culture and habits, acquainting societies with cultural and religious customs and picking advantages of source target cultures.

Cultural translation which is carried out by the media plays a vital role in making a culture universal and general. It acts as a bridge to communicate all kinds of languages specially those similar to each other considering their linguistic features and cultural customs in all parts of the world (Zimmerman, 2012). So it links all units of the world in the global network.

Since translation transfers the culture, unconsciously behind this culture, we get familiar with the pop cultures and people's habits of different regions (IPEDR, 2012). IPEDR (2012) gives the example of "Mother Day" as a pop culture that shows pop cultures and people's habits of different regions. They quip that "Mother Day" as a pop culture shows that people respect Mothers. So this special day has become a habit for all countries in different geographical regions. 'Valentine' as pop culture has been adopted literally by all people of the world. This has had an impact due to the media and the way they translate global issues.

Each society propagates its own specific culture through translation (Byram, 1989). Culture translation helps to know the variety of worship of different cultures. For e.g. Muslim pray in Mosque, Christian in Church, Jewish in Synagogue. Celebrating "Christmas Day" has been expanded. Thus, translation link cultures as a chain. Thus translation obviously is a cross-cultural communication. This is heavily carried out by journalists who translate these religious activities to different languages of the world and communicate values and vices.

A proper translation makes the reader to ponder over the cultural context of the source language (Larson, 1988). Cultural borrowing is one of the advantages that transfer ideas, customs, and social behaviors from another culture. By an adequate translation, readers or audience of target language culture will acquire a lot of useful benefits for e.g. how they relate with elders, dressing, hospitality and etiquette through translation. This engages media to communicate these values exactly using the meaning based translation.

Language Typology

Language typology is the investigation of linguistic types. Linguistic typology is a cross-linguistic description and explanation of the unity and diversity of languages with respect to linguistic form or the relation between linguistic form and meaning/function (Croft, 2003). Different languages display different linguistic typologies in the various fields of linguistics. Catford (1974) states that it is almost impossible for translators to produce a TT which is grammatically and lexically identical to the ST, and this is because languages differ in the way they use lexical and grammatical devices in order to express meaning. Linguistic typology are grouped into three broad categories that consist of smaller types. Whaley (1997) tabulates them as follows;

Morphological

This includes; isolating, synthesis, polysynthetic, fissional and agglutinative

Morphosyntactic

This includes - alignment, accusative, ergative, split ergative, Philippine, active- stative, tripartite, inverse marking, syntactic pivot and theta role

Word order

This includes; VO languages such as subject verb object, verb subject object; OV languages such as subject object verb, object subject verb, object verb subject; time manner place and place manner time.

Not all of the above linguistic typologies and their influence on translation will be discussed in this chapter. But a few will do for the purposes of elaboration. We may pick one from each category or pick the most problematic in translation in various languages of the world.

Pischedda (2013) observed the following problems of translation regarding linguistic typology between English and Italian. First, compound words in English when translated to Italian tend to form new words in Italian. This is because Italian Language assumes an analytical syntactical structure. This being the case, the Italian Language introduces prepositions to relate elements of English Language. Pischedda illustrated this translation problem using the following;

English- 'chimps' a four-page, Gregg Heffley

Italian- 'scimmiette' UN tema **di** Quattro pagine **di** Gregg Heffley

He argues that the two languages grammatical structures lack grammatical equivalence.

Another translation problem caused by linguistic typology between English and Italian is onomatopoeic sounds. In English, onomatopoeic sounds end in consonants because of their imitative purpose. However, Pischedda (2003) notes that in Italian onomatopoeic sounds end in vowels because of their need to express categories of gender and number through the addition of suffices. Moreover, they are often longer due to Latin influence.

Under morphological linguistic typology category, we wish to discuss the agglutinating and fissional languages type. This is because it is significant as a translation problem and cuts across many languages. Agglutinating and fusional language typologies both have words formed by morphemes. The only difference is, with agglutinating, you can tell where one morpheme begins and ends while, with fusional, you can't. This is because while agglutinating morphemes have one meaning for one morpheme, fusional means there are many meanings in one morpheme (Croft, 2002).

Under word order linguistic typology category, we have some languages that split verbs into an auxiliary and an infinitive or participle, and put the subject and/or object between them (Song, 2001). Song, (2001) observed that, German ("Im Wald *habe* ich einen Fuchs *gesehen*" - "In-the woods have I a fox seen"), Dutch ("Hans *vermoedde* dat Jan Piet Marie *zag leren zwemmen*" - "Hans suspected that Jan Piet Marie saw teach swim") and Welsh ("*Mae*'r gwirio sillafu wedi'i *gwblhau*" - "Is the checking spelling after its to complete"). In this case, typology is based on the non-analytic tenses (i.e. those sentences in which the verb is not split) or the position of the auxiliary. German is thus SVO/VSO (without "im Wald" the agent would go first) in main clauses and Welsh is VAP (and P would go after the infinitive). Having an isomorphic translation from one language to the other would be so difficult with this kind of a linguistic typology.

Further, under morphosyntactic linguistic typology category, many languages show mixed accusative and ergative behaviour. For example, ergative morphology marking the verb arguments, on top of an accusative syntax (Cysouw, 2005). Other languages, active languages, have two types of intransitive verbs—some of them, active verbs, join the subject in the same case as the agent of a transitive verb, and the rest "stative verbs" join the subject in the same case as the patient. Yet other languages behave ergatively only in some contexts. This is called split ergativity, and is usually based on the grammatical person of the arguments or in the tense/aspect of the verb (Cysouw, 2005). Mixed accusative and ergative behavior of languages renders translation of world languages difficult. There is more on problems of translation of world languages posed by linguistic typology but for the purposes of this chapter that will suffice.

Genre

Genre refers to different categories of literal texts or different styles of writing. In a globalized world, translating different genres could present hefty difficulties translators. This is because, the written languages carry societal values and vices that are passed in figurative language. According to Wray (2002), psycholinguistics has shown us that idiomatic multiword units may cause difficulties in identification and comprehension. They have a holistic meaning because they are stored and retrieved whole from memory with their associated meaning and form. Naciscione (2006) in her study of figurative translation in Latvia observed a number of a challenges. One, translators tended to demetaphorise figurative terms in a bid to arrive to a close translation. She offers this example; 'the process owner' has been translated into 'the process director', which is not only a semantic and stylistic loss but it also inhibits comprehension and causes misunderstandings (2006: 105). Most figurative words are defined or explained because they fail to meet an equivalent translation. A definition of a metaphorical term is dysfunctional in practice. It does not lend itself to derivative and phrase formation either. It is not flexible in text, and the translation of the term creates serious syntactic and stylistic problems (2006: 109).

Ecology

Ecology is a biological term. It refers to the relationship of organisms to their surroundings. Physical surrounding varies from one place to place. This is dependent on the geographical factors of the place. Inhabitants of a certain geographical setting identify with factors that prevail like weather circumstances and the dressing code that is convenient with the weather, plants that grow in the area, food that the environment offers and animals that condone the weather conditions. Does translation have anything to do with ecology? The source texts (ST) may display environmental terms that are not found in the target text (TT) (Nida, 1981). For instance, the Bible relates very well with the Palestinian environment. Translations to other languages fail to relate to some issues due to the orientation and varied terminologies that envisages those environments. Communicating this information to the globalized world through translation becomes a challenge.

Language Dynamism

Language dynamism refer to the changes that language under go over time. There are many factors that contribute to changes in language but will not be discussed in this chapter because it is not the focus of this chapter. Our focus is on how language dynamism influence translation in a globalized world. As media seek for information to communicate to their audiences, they need to check on the changes the languages they undergo in order to make adjustments in their translations. We have two types of language dynamics; internal and external (Aitchison, 1991). "Internal language dynamics" refer to the processes through which any language is liable to change. Morphosyntax and phonology. Evolve over time Change can remain slow over extended periods of time, but it may also suddenly accelerate in response to particular conjunction of factors (Aitchson, 1991). External language dynamics refer to all processes of language spread, maintenance and decline, and because these dynamics, necessarily concern the respective position of different languages with respect to each other (Bauer & Trudgill, 1998).

In Kenya, our ethnic languages have been undergoing a lot of dynamism especially due to the influence of Sheng. In all spheres of life, political, religious, social etc sheng has been embraced as it is widely used by the youth (Githiora, 2002). Since the youth are the majority people in the society, the elderly are turning to using sheng either to reach the youth or to conform. Recently, during the political campaigns, the aspirants for various posts were seen to use sheng in a bid to win the youth. For instance, a slogan like 'tunawesmake', coined by Peter Kenneth appealed heavily to the youth. Most other aspirants were heard using sheng during their campaign rallies. The church has not been left behind in this influence. Their summons are symbolized by sheng language usage which are geared towards holding and retaining the youth in church. Translators are tasked with difficulties when translating from one language to another. This is because sheng does not belong to either the SL or the TL. Sheng picks its vocabulary from various languages Ogechi, 2005). Besides, it lacks structure and differ from one place to another (Momanyi, 2009).

Why Translate World Languages?

Globalization has reduced the world into a global village. This has opened doors for interactions in various fields. Manenji (1998) observes that globalization has opened up the world for trade to all by liberalizing it. The need for world peoples to interact economically, academically, politically, socially and spiritually through the technologically available channels that have reduced cost on both communication and transport (Pym, 2003) necessitates for linguistic intelligibility. Besides, world peoples have accepted to adopt to world cultures especially in areas of entertainment and eating habits. Most countries have introduced the use of English language, which is the widely used language in the world termed as the 'world's lingua franca' to allow intelligibility. For countries adamant to introduce the use of English language, it has become mandatory to translate English language into their local languages (Newmark, 1998). This deems it highly necessary to translate world languages.

More specifically, translation in a globalized world is important for companies which operate in multiple countries. They need to pass information or collect data from all the employees or branches across the world. It is also important for external affairs of a nation. World leaders are expected to present their ideas on situations arising in other parts of the world. It is important that those ideas are translated properly when expressed, else they can result in major catastrophe (Ginsburgh, Weber & Weyers, 2007).

The need to interchange culture also makes translation in a globalized world important. Art forms like music, films and literature from a region is necessary for global understanding of a region and its life. For example, the plight of Palestine refugees, the poverty in Brazilian streets, the colourful life in Spanish cities and the myths and legends of ancient India are spreading across the world, riding on the shoulder of good translation (Larson, 1998). (Shuttleworth & Moiro, 2007) observe that translated films and subtitled films generate more revenue for global film industry, while translated music and literature provides added royalties to artistes.

Transference of News on world events is another importance of translation in a globalized world. Unless proper translation on News is done, the news may be ambiguous and unreliable. Sometimes, we have nations that refuse international news coverage especially when they want to cover up internal problems. This can be seen when the government of China recently banned international news agencies from entering local regions to cover major problems encountered (Bermann & Wood, 2007). Bermann & Wood (2007) retaliates that information was still passed on to the world because insiders covered all the important news, translated it and presented it to the world.

Bermann & Wood (2007) states that global citizenship can only be achieved through sharing and caring. There is need to communicate our ideas and thoughts. Different people around the world use different languages. They are comfortable handling their online activities in their own regional languages which they translate their thoughts in English to enable their global friends understand them (Gentzler, 1993).

Boost of tourism will require proper translation around the globe. Tourists around the world complain of being short-changed and tricked as they are unfamiliar with the destination (Bermann & Wood, 2007). These negative experiences are drawn by lack of proper translation. When adequate translations are offered to tourists, a country enjoys popularity as a tourist destination and also helps increasing the country's revenue.

Role of Translation in a Globalized World

Translation in the world can have both negative and positive effects (Newmark, 2003). It can cause great harm in form of conflict and even war. At the same time, it can create wealth and harmony in the world. This section discusses the role of translation in a globalized world.

Advantages of Translation in a Globalized World

Translation in a globalized world enjoys more good than harm. Although globalization has been blamed for eroding small cultures by forcing them to adopt to norms not beneficial to them (Miasami, 2003), Moussalli (2003) affirms that one of the functions of translation in a globalized world is being a promoter of the integration of the world cultures minus cultural barriers leaving these cultures to face competition and challenges of the modern technologies and innovations. Wiersema (2004) looks at globalization as a process that allows cultures to collaborate and interact with flexibility while exotising is a helping hand to translation. He further remarks, "In our globalized world, translation is the key to understanding and learning foreign cultures".

Translation in a globalized world serves as a unifying factor. When information is adequately translated from one language to another, people tend to understand each other. They share opinions and hence view things from the same perspective. This common ground shared by people from various parts of the world enhances unity. Translation in a globalized world is important as it serves as a profession. In this era of unemployment, many people have found themselves jobs in translation. Many people feed and support their families through earnings made from translating languages from one to the other. It also serves as a business. Firms have been set up to facilitate translation. In fact, translation businesses are lucrative with many people running for them.

Translation in a globalized world serves to spread the gospel. Warren (2002) states that in the book of Revelation, God's mission is to have the gospel spread in the whole globe. Metzger (2003) notes that the Bible has been translated into more languages than any other piece of literature. This is in a bid to spread the gospel in as many parts of the world as possible.

Conclusion

Translation in a globalized world brings on board a number of issues as envisaged in this account. First, definitions of major terminologies like translation and globalization was done. The role of media in translation in a globalized world took a centre stage as they try to inform global masses on the unfolding in diverse fields. Issues in translation in a globalized world have also been explored that include culture, language typology, genre, ecology, language dynamism and technology. All these tend to affect translation in one way or the other. The reasons why translation should be done across world languages was discussed which unearthed salient issues. The role of translation in a globalized world came lastly which was seen to carry two sides of a coin; negative and positive side. It was found to cause harm some harm especially when there is mistranslation. All the same, it was found to have more advantages than harm. For instance, it was found to foster unity in the world, promote the integration of cultures, source of employment and a tool to spread the gospel.

References

Aitchison, J. (1991). Language Change: Progress or Decay? Cambridge. Cambridge University Press.

Bauer, L. and Trudgill, P. (1998). Language Myths. London: Penguin.

Bermann, S. and Wood, M. (2007) ed. Nation, Language and the Ethics of Translation Princeton. Princeton University Press.

Byram, M. (1989). Cultural Studies in Foreign Language Education. Clenedon: Multilingual Matters.

Carlson, E.D. (2001). A Case Study in Translation Methodology Using the Health- Promotion Lifestyle Profile. Public Health Nurs.

Croft, W. (2003). Tyopology and Universals. 2nd ed. Cambridge: Cambridge University Press.

Croft, W. (2002). Typology and Universals. Cambridge. UP.

Cysouw, M. (2005). Quantitative Methods of Typology. Quantitative Linguistics: an International Handbook, ed. Gabriel Altman, Reinhard Kohler and R. Protrowski. Berlin: Mouton de Gruyter.

Gentzeler, E. (1993). Contemporary Translation Theories. London. Routledge.

Ginsburgh, V., Weber, S. and Weyers, S. (2007). The Economics of Literary Translation A Simple Theory of Evidence, CEPR Discussion Chapter, 6432, August 2007.

Githiora, C. (2002). Sheng: Peer Language, Swahili Dialect or Emerging Creole? Journal of African Cultural Studies. London: Routledge.

Graffi, G. and Scalise, S. (2003). Le Lingue eil Linguaggio: Introduzione alla Lingui Bologona: Il Mulino.

Hymes, D. (2000). Ed. Languages in Culture and Society. Reader in Linguistics and Anthropology. New York. Harper and Row.

IPEDR (2012). International Conference on Language, Media and Culture. Vol, 33 IACSIT Press. Singapore.

Larson, L.M. (1998). Meaning–Based Translation. A Guide to Cross-Language Equivalence. New York. University Press of America.

Manenji, F.M. (1998). The Effects of Globalization on Culture in the Eyes of an Africa Woman. www.oikoumene.org/resources. Downloaded on 27/10/2013.

Metzger, B.M. (1993). Important Early Translations of the Bible. www.faculty.gordon.edu.

Miasami, M. "Islam and Globalization" in Fountain, August 2003.

Momanyi, C. (2009). The Effects of Sheng in the Teaching of Kiswahili in Kenyan Schools. The Journal of African Studies, Vol.2, no.8.

Moussalli, M. "Impact of Globalization" in Daily Star, August 21, 2003.

Naciscione, A. (2006). Figurative Language in Translation: A Cognitive Approach Cognitive Terms. In Pragmatics Aspects of Translation (ed.A. Veisbergs); Proceedings of the Font Riga International Symposium. Riga: University Of Latvia, National Language Commission: 102-118.

Newmark, P. (2003). Translation in a Globalized World. New York. Prentice Hall.

Newmark, P. (1988). A Textbook of Translation. New York. Prentice Hall.

Nida, E.A. (1981). From One Language to Another. Functional Equivalence in Bible Translation. Tennessee: Thomas Nelson Publishers.

Nida, E.A. and Reybum, W.D. (1981). Meaning Across Cultures. New York. Obis Books.

Ogechi, N. (2005). On Lexicalization in Sheng. Nordic Journal of African Studies. 14(3) 334-355.

Okrent, A. (2013). 9 Little Translation Mistakes that Caused Big Problems.

Mentalfloss.com/ Article/48795/9. Downloaded on 25/10/2013.

Pischedda, P.S. (2013). Handling Typological Differences in English-Italian Translations. University of Leeds. www.academia.edu/2075122. Downloaded on 23/10/2013.

Pym, A. (2003). Globalization and Politics in Translation Studies. Manchester, St. Jerome Publishing.

Rosenfelder, M. (2012). The Language Construct Kit. www.zompist.com/kitgram.html Downloaded 23/10/2013.

Samuel, P. and Frank, D. (2000). Translating Poetry and Figurative Language into St. Lucian Creole. www. Saintluciancreole. Downloaded on 23/10/2013.

Shibatani, M. and Bynon, T. (1995). Ed. Approaches to Language. Oxford: Claredon Press.

Shuttleworth, M. and Moiro, C. (2007). Dictionary of Translation Studies. Manchester: St. Jerome Publishing.

Song, J.J. (2001). Linguistic Typology: Morphology and Syntax. Harlow and London: Pearson Education (Longman).

Venuti, L. (2002). On the Different Methods of Translating. The Translation Studies.Readers London, Routledge.

Venuti, L. (1994). The Translator's Invisibility. London. Routledge.

Warren, R. (2002). The Purpose Driven Life. Oasis International Ltd. Michigan.

Whaley, L.J. (1997). Introduction to Typology: The Unity and Diversity of Language. Newbury. Sage.

Wiersema, N. (2004). Globalization and Translation: A Discussion of the Effect of Gobalization on Today's Translation. Translation Journal, Vol.8, No. 1.

Wilson, A. (2009). Translators on Translating: inside the Invisible Art. Vancouver: CCSP Press.

Zimmerman, K.A. (2012). What is Culture? Definition of Culture. www.livescience.com 21478. Downloaded on 21/10/2013

Chapter Eight
Lexical Ambiguity of Homonymy and Polysemy in Ekegusii
S. Onchoke Aunga

Introduction

Diction plays a key role in communication especially where different categories of people communication process. However, if diction is not used well it can lead to breakdown of communication or no communication at all. This is so because some words are ambiguous, that is, they have more than one meaning. Polysemy and homonymy is true example of lexical ambiguity in any language. The purpose of this chapter is to identify and analyze homonymous and polysemous sense relations in a minority language, Ekegusii. The two sense relations are problematic and confusing as seen from the studies conducted in the Indo-European family of languages like English. This chapter is based on the premise that the two sense relations are also problematic in Ekegusii, an African Bantu minority language spoken in Kenya. The research objectives are: to identify and explain words that have more than one meaning; to determine the extent to which polysemous words can be distinguished from homonymous ones in and lastly, to establish the extent to which polysemy and homonymy in Ekegusii can be accounted for within the Sense Relations Theory. The Sense Relations Theory forms the theoretical framework used to account for the data. This chapter is part of a study carried out in Nyamira County where there are Ekegusii native speakers. The study used an interview schedule to collect information from 20 elderly native Ekegusii speakers of between 50 and 70 years of age who were chosen using judgemental sampling technique. Their intuitions about the relatedness or otherwise of words with more than one meaning were captured and analyzed within the Sense Relations Theory. The study findings revealed that there are Ekegusii words with multiple meanings; some of these words are as a result of the process of borrowing. Drawing a distinction between homonymous and polysemous words, sometimes, can be very difficult. The study, therefore, concluded that the two terms are confusing and ambiguous. The study contributes to the field of lexical semantics and so related studies may find the information it provides relevant for reference. Finally, research findings will provide information necessary for further discovery on how language operates in line with Kenya's vision of 2030, with emphasis on highlighting the role of social science research particularly in local minority languages such as Ekegusii in promoting translation and economic development.

This chapter carries out a lexical semantics study of the nature of homonymous and polysemous sense relations in Ekegusii. According to Guthrie (1964), Ekegusii, whose speakers are called Abagusii, are labeled zone E42 narrow East African Bantu language group, occupying the southern section of the cool and fertile western highlands of Kenya.

According to Palmer (1981), semantics is a relatively recent branch of linguists which appeared in the late 19th century. It has been defined variously by different writers. Fasold and Connor- Semantics has two main branches: one is formal semantics, also called sentence semantics, which deals with how components of a complex expression interact and combine; two, lexical semantics, which is also referred to as word meaning and it deals with meanings stored in the mental lexicon (Cruse, 2000). The latter is the concern of this chapter.

Saeed (1997:53) posits that the traditional descriptive aim of lexical semantics has been to:

(a) Represent the meaning of each word in a language.
(b) Show how the meanings of words in a language are interrelated.

Saeed further states that the meaning of a word is defined in part by it relations with other words in the language. The semantic relations are central to the way speakers and hearers construct meaning. These relations, which hold between lexical items, are called lexical relations or sense relations. The different sense relations which exist between different linguistic units are: Synonymy (lexemes sharing similar sense), antonymy (lexemes with senses opposed to each other), hyponymy (sense of one lexeme included in the sense of another), metonymy (relationship between part and whole), metonymy (a relationship where one entity stands for another associated entity), homonymy (unrelated sense of the same word) and polysemy (related sense of the same word). The concern of this study is to examine the lexical ambiguities presented in homonymy and polysemy in Ekegusii, a Bantu language.

According to Keith (1986), something is ambiguous when it can be understood in two or more possible ways or when it has more than one meaning. If the ambiguity is occasioned by the arrangement of words in a sentence or clause, it is called structural (syntactic) ambiguity. If it is in a single word, it is called lexical ambiguity. He notes that lexical semantic ambiguity occurs when a single word is associated with multiple senses. Lexical ambiguity can refer to both homonymy and polysemy. This is what this chapter focuses on.

Richards (1993:240) observes that our languages are cornerstones of who we are as a people. Language loss is part of a much larger process of loss of cultural and intellectual diversity in which politically dominant languages and cultures overwhelm indigenous local languages. This situation is worse if the latter are not in print.

Indeed, a survey of the literature available shows that studies on lexical semantics based on African indigenous languages are not as many as those on the Indo-European family of languages. Further, it is evident that there is hardly any work on semantics in Ekegusii, a Bantu minority language in Kenya and other Kenyan indigenous languages in general.

A Brief History of Semantics, Ambiguity, Homonymy and Polysemy

Keith (1986) observes that the meaning of a word is determined by its use in a language. This meaning can be revealed by whoever coins it by defining it formally or it can be figured from the context of use. He identifies three kinds of meaning: sense; the property of meaning in abstract categories such as a sentence, phrase, lexeme and morpheme, denotation; the use of sense in speaking of some particular world and utterance meaning; what the hearer rationally determines that a speaker intends his meaning to convey. He stresses further that sense is central in determining other kinds of meaning. This chapter focuses on sense as the property of meaning in Ekegusii lexemes.

Kempson (1977) adds by stating that there may be disagreement about the fine details of the meaning of words 'around the edges,' found in the everyday use of language but all words are understood by speakers as having an indispensable hard core of meaning. For example, the meaning of 'cat' includes that of animal, the meaning of 'adult' excludes the meaning of child, the meaning of 'kill' is related to that of dead in such a way that anything killed is necessarily dead. The meanings of lexical items are stated in terms of their entailments. This means that every lexeme and sentence is conventionally associated with at least one meaning. This chapter assumes also that an Ekegusii word has at least one meaning but is interested in those that have more than one meaning.

Graddal and Swan (1989:97) posit that the study of meaning relies on people's intuition about language; the intuitions of ordinary natural speakers, researchers, and lexicographers, which researchers use as sources. Problems arise because different people's intuitions do not always agree and because different peoples' intuitions of how a word or expression should be used do not always coincide with how they actually use it. This chapter borrows a leaf from this observation because it relies on native speakers' intuitions about meaning in getting the meanings of the target words and determining whether they are homonymous or polysemous lexemes and draw a distinction between them.

Palmer (1990) asserts that the test of polysemy is through relatedness and word etymology. Etymological information is the lexicographer's knowledge of the historical derivation of words. Relatedness is how close the meanings are (which is very subjective). He says that if two senses of the same word do not seem to fit, yet, seem related, then it is likely that they are polysemous. This chapter is synchronic and so it does not rely on etymologies.

Wierzbicka (1996:244) argues that the lexicographers will do well to reckon always with polysemy because it is problematic and will cause one to undertake very deep analysis of the words' meanings. He adds that lexicographers, when writing dictionaries, often posit a great deal of unjustified polysemy and also frequently fail to recognize polysemy which is really there. He acknowledges the fact that polysemes are single lexemes and are treated as single entries in a dictionary.

Frath (2002:57) captures the dilemma that the lexicographers face in their treatment of lexical ambiguity. He notes that dictionaries consist of out of context words and that some dictionaries lump homonyms together and others separate polysemes, which may be an indication that the boundary between polysemy and homonymy is not clear cut. In other words, if you hear (or read) two words that sound (or are written) the same but are not identical in meaning, you need to decide if it's really two words (homonyms), or if it is one word used in two different ways (polysemy). He emphasizes that the only real way we have of telling the two apart is by applying our judgement. He argues further that there are no tests that can tell them apart in a foolproof manner.

Lyons (1990, 550) posits that there are only two ways of distinguishing between homonymy and polysemy: word etymology and relatedness and unrelatedness of meaning. Etymological information (lexicographer's knowledge of the historical derivation of words) is employed by linguists and lexicographers to come to decision about Homonymy and polysemy. For homonymy, the lexemes in question should be known to have developed from what were formally distinct lexemes in some earlier stages of the language.

According to Lyons (1990:550), the second area of distinction between homonymy and polysemy is unrelatedness versus relatedness in meaning. He argues that traditionally linguists and lexicographers use this criterion in drawing the distinction between homonymy and polysemy, and it is the only synchronically relevant consideration. It is about the native speaker's feelings that certain meanings are connected and that others are not. He asserts strongly that relatedness of meaning appears to be a matter of degree and it has yet to be demonstrated, so, the descriptive semanticist should take into account of the native speakers' intuitions of relatedness of meaning in deciding between homonymy and polysemy. This chapter benefits from Lyon's work because relies on the native speakers' intuitions about meanings, relatedness and unrelatedness of the polysemous and homonymous sense relations to draw a distinction between them.

Theoretical Framework

The chapter is anchored on the Sense Relations Theory as postulated by Gottlob (1892) and expounded by Lyons (2005), Keith (1986), Kempson (1977), Palmer (1986, 1996 & 2000), Lobner (2002), Pustejovsky (1980 & 1995), Cann (1993), Katz (2004), Cruse (1986 & 2000) and Davis & Gillion (2004).

The Sense Relations Theory was first associated with the Germany philosopher and mathematician Gottlob Frege in his 1892 chapter *Ober Sinn Und Bedeutung* (on sense and reference). According to Frege, sense and reference are two different aspects of the meaning of at least some kind of terms. The sense of a term is the way in which it refers to the object. He argued further that a word's sense is one of the meanings of a word. The sense of a proper name is whatever meaning it has, when there is no object to be indicated. He posited that sense is the cognitive significance or mode of presentation of the referent. The sense of an expression is that wherein the mode of presentation is contained.

The lexical relations (patterns of association that exist between lexical items in a language, also seen as the tenets of this theory) that the Sense Relations Theory covers are: homonymy which means unrelated senses of the same word. For instance, in English the word *bark* refers to the noise made by a dog and the outer part of a tree. Synonymy refers to sharing a similar sense. In English, for example, the words *reject* and *refuse*, are almost similar in their senses. Polysemy is another concept which refers to related senses of the same word. For instance, the English word *eat* in the Kenyan context could have many related senses; *swallow food, take a bribe or misappropriate funds*. Antonymy refers to senses opposed to each other. For example, in English, the words *dead and alive* are opposite in their senses. Meronymy refers to the sense of between part and whole, where the part is called meronym and the whole, a holonym. In the case of *hand and finger,* hand is the holonym and finger is a meronym respectively. Hyponymy refers to the sense of one word being included in the sense of another. Here the umbrella term is referred to as the hyponym or super-ordinate term and the one that is under is referred to as hyponym. For example, *mango and orange* are hyponyms of the term *fruit* which is a super ordinate term or hyponym. The last concept is metonymy which refers to a relationship where one entity stands for another associated identity. For example, somebody with an abnormally big head could be referred to as *head*. These relations are given a detailed discussion by the proponents of this theoretical framework (Cann, 1993), (Palmer, 1996), (Lyons, 1995), (Kearns, 2000), (Cruse, 1995), (Hurford & Hearseley, 1983), (Kempson, 1977) and (Pustejovsky, 1995).

The sense relations theory is useful in the identification and analysis of homonymous and polysemous sense relations in Ekegusii. For instance, it informs the study that the term *bwatia* which is a verb in Ekegusii with two unrelated meanings: (a) to follow and (b) to warm something like water. The two meanings have nothing in common in terms of meaning, but have the same pronunciation and spelling hence the word is a total homonym. In an Ekegusii dictionary, it would be given two lexical entries. The term *saba* is another verb in Ekegusii with more than three related senses (a) ask, (b) pray and (c) seduce somebody. The meanings have something in common, *ask,* can be taken to be the core meaning. The other two meanings are related in that, pray, is to ask God for something, while to seduce is to ask for a sexual favour. These meanings can be said to stem from the core meaning *ask,* hence, secondary or derived. In an Ekegusii dictionary, lexicographers would treat it as a single lexeme; therefore, it is a polyseme.

Research Methodology

The chapter adopted a qualitative research design. It seeks to describe phenomena that occur naturally without the intervention of an experiment or artificially contrived treatment (Seligar and Shohamy, 1989).

The study population would have potentially entailed all Ekegusii speakers. The study limited itself to 20 informants proficient in the native language comprising adults of between 50 and 70 years of age, born and brought up in Kisii. They were chosen from the many using judgemental sampling technique, taking into account the variable of gender to avoid bias. The informants included 10 men and 10 women. This small sample was chosen in order to allow for in-depth investigation and analysis of data (Trudgill, 1973).

The researcher identified a researcher assistant to guide him to suitable respondents and help in the recording of the respondents☐ intuitions about meanings of the lexemes given. The list of 20 words which were subjected to the respondents were sampled by the researcher using judgemental sampling on the basis that they had more than one meaning. The other 80 words with multiple meanings were sampled from the many generated by the respondents in the field by using stratified random sampling. The number of the targeted sense relations and word classes in each category were determined after doing the sampling. In total the researcher had 100 words with multiple meanings to analyze. The study utilized an interview schedule where the respondents were subjected to the same questions and grouped according to the variable of gender. The interview schedule had open ended questions which permitted a greater depth of response which in turn gave an insight into the feelings, background, hidden motivation, intuitions, interests and decisions of the respondents (Mugenda and Mugenda, 1999). The interview schedule had a list of polysemes and homonyms which the researcher had identified. The respondents were required, using their intuitions and memory, to say if the words had multiple meanings, describe the meanings, say if the meanings were related or not and generate more examples of words with multiple meanings. Primary data sources were used. The researcher, being an Ekegusii native speaker, identified words with multiple meanings in Ekegusii using his memory and intuition about meaning. The list contained 20 words. The rest were generated in the field by the respondents. The interview method was used whereby the researcher came face to face with the subjects using an interview schedule (Seliger and Shohamy, 1990). The list was presented to the respondents who were equally proficient speakers of Ekegusii to provide the different meanings of a given word and then said if the meanings were related or not. Then the respondents generated more examples of words with multiple meanings in Ekegusii. The data was recorded by the researcher and the researcher assistant for accuracy. The data collected was non-numerical (words) which was analyzed qualitatively. After identifying the lexical items under consideration (homonymous and polysemous lexemes), the data was transcribed and translated into English. The analysis of data was discursive, that is, the researcher identified, delimited and sorted the relevant segments of the information, calculated percentages and represented the information in pie charts, then, drew logical deductions in relation to the behavior of the analyzed data. The words and their multiple meanings were sorted out as given and explained by the respondents. The researcher then synthesized the meanings accordingly and wrote the summaries for each particular item. Based on the information from the summaries of meanings for each word, a distinction between homonyms and polysemes was made. By focusing on a particular lexical item, the researcher examined the informants' intuitions and his own to decide where a lexical item fell. Lastly, the analyzed data was subjected to the tenets of The Sense Relations Theory to gauge the extent to which the theory could have accounted for polysemy and homonymy in Ekegusii.

Results and Discussion

The data that was collected from 20 competent Ekegusii native respondents comprised 300 words with multiple meanings. Basing on the Sense Relations Theory, the words were classified into homonyms and polysemes by the researcher. There were 80 homonyms and 220 polysemes. The polysemes were identified by the criteria that they have related meanings and that one meaning was thought of as literal meaning and the others as extended meanings that are derived from the first (Greenbaum, 1996).

On the other hand, homonyms were identified on the basis that they are ambiguous words whose different senses are far apart from each other and not obviously related to each other in any way (Hurford and Hearsley, 1989).

From the list of words, there are those that the respondents found problematic to classify whether the meanings are related or not and there are those whose status they agreed on unanimously. The controversial ones were explained first then the explicit ones followed later. Tables and pie charts were used to aid the presentation of the responses obtained.

The figure that follows gives a summary of words with multiple meanings as collected from the respondents.

Fig. 1: Summary of words with multiple meanings in Ekegusii

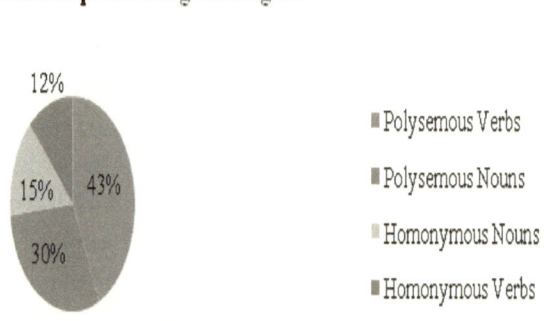

Figure 1 shows that a total of 300 words with multiple meanings were collected from the respondents. Basing on the sense relations theory, the words were classified into homonyms and polysemes. There were 220 polysemes and 80 homonyms. Out of the 220 polysemes, were 130 verbs representing 43%, and 90 nouns representing 30%. Out of the 80 homonyms, 45 representing 15% were nouns and 35 verbs representing 12%. This brings out the fact that verbs tend to be polysemous and nouns tend to be homonymous. Example of a polysemous verb is *bereka*.

Bereka has the sense of **carrying on the back** as happens when one is carrying a baby or heavy luggage. *'bereka'* can also refer to **the flowering of a maize plant**. This is evident when a maize plant starts producing or forming a cob. It is like the maize plant is carrying some weight. The third sense is **carrying rumors from one person and place to another**. A person spreading rumors is seen metaphorically as carrying some load. The three senses share the concept of weight being carried at some place. The meanings are related, hence making the word, a polyseme.

The researcher then did a stratified random sampling to come up with 100 words with multiple meanings, 50 homonyms and 50 polysemes. In each group are 25 nouns and 25 verbs.

The figure below gives a summary.

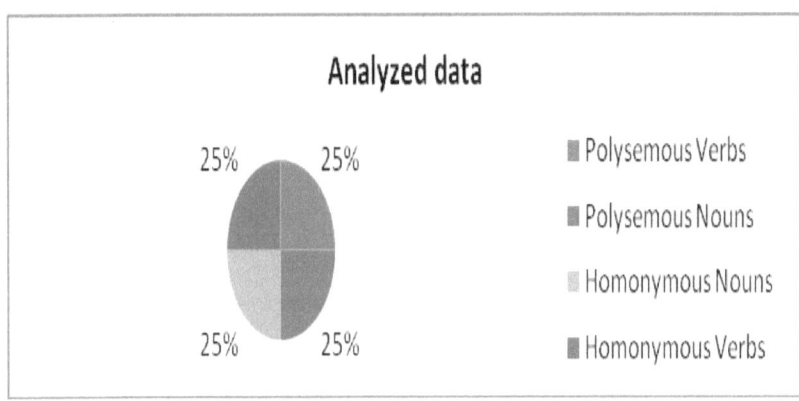

Fig. 2: Analyzed words with multiple meanings in Ekegusii

This chapter is part of a study that sought to identify and explain Ekegusii words that have more than one meaning, determine the extent to which polysemous words can be distinguished from homonymous ones in Ekegusii and finally, to establish the extent to which homonymy and polysemy in Ekegusii can be accounted for within the Sense Relations Theory.

The result of our investigation reveals that to a large extent, the assumptions of the study are confirmed. In Ekegusii, words with multiple meanings exist. Out of the 300 words with multiple meaning collected from the respondents, 274, representing 91.3%, have two meanings each, 25, representing 8.3%, have 3 meanings each and 1, representing 0.3%, has 5 meanings. Example of a word with five meanings. Greenbaum (1996) postulates that homonyms are considered coincidental, few and are a defect in any language. The research findings confirm this to some extent. Out of the 300 words with multiple meanings collected from the respondents, 80 turned out to be homonyms and 220 polysemes but this categorization was not without controversy.

Language and Translation

The study also shows that the frequently used words in Ekegusii tend to be more polysemic than the less frequently used just as in the case in other languages (Greenbaum, 1996). For example, the term *amache*, has the literal meaning of **water.** The other extended meanings are: **urine, alcohol, male reproductive fluid and beer.** All these meanings have one thing in common: they are liquids. Water is commonly used and without it there is no life. No wonder it was able to attract several references from the respondents.

The chapter reveals that sometimes it is not easy to distinguish between homonymy and polysemy. In the course of the research, the respondents, using their intuitions about meaning sometimes, could not agree on whether a word was a polyseme or a homonym. This prompted the researcher to use the criterion of relatedness and un-relatedness, metaphor, ambiguity test and the general knowledge of the sense relations in order to make a decision. This is illustrated by the following examples:

Rigena is a noun with three meanings, a stone, an egg and a hailstone. The first two meanings, according to the respondents, are not related. The third meaning, hailstone, is related to that of a stone. Among the Abagusii, hailstones are specifically referred to as *amagena ye embura,* meaning "stones of the rain" because of their shapes. A stone and an egg elicited different responses from the respondents. There were some respondents who felt that there is a connection between the first two meanings because some stones take the shape of an egg; therefore, the word should be treated as a polyseme. Others felt that there is no connection between the two meanings. A bigger percentage of the twenty respondents, using their intuitions about meaning, felt that it is a homonym. This situation is echoed by Graddal and Swan (1989) who posit that the study of meaning relies on people's intuition about language-the intuitions of ordinary natural speakers, researchers, and lexicographers, which researchers use as sources. Problems arise because different people's intuitions do not always agree and because different peoples' intuitions of how a word or expression should be used do not always coincide with how they actually use it.

Those respondents who felt that the word is a polyseme were 8, representing 40%, while those that said it is a homonym were 12, representing 60%. The percentages are presented in figure 3

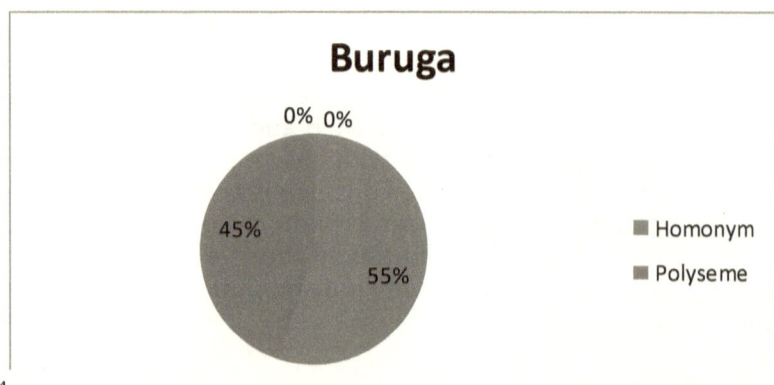

Fig. 3: Respondents' classification of *rigena*

From the pie chart above, we can see that the majority of the respondents felt that the word is a homonym. We also felt that the word is a homonymy because there are clear differences in meaning. Whereas the stone is associated with hardness, takes no particular shape, and is rough, an egg, on the other hand, is associated with fragility or delicateness, has an oval shape and is smooth.

'Buruga' is another Ekegusii verb which is also ambiguous. It has two meanings, one being **to weed crops** (e.g. maize, beans or millet) and the other **to stir something** (e.g. ugali or uji or tea) when cooking. Some respondents felt that it should be treated as a polyseme because both senses contain the concept of an action and that weeding and stirring are related. In both, the stirring is meant to achieve a certain positive effect clear the crops of the weeds so as to grow healthy and make the fluid substance thicken to the desired consistency. We also, using our intuitions about meaning, could not establish an obvious conceptual connection between the two meanings and that one can't easily pick the core and the peripheral meanings. This is not surprising given that it is not always clear whether one is dealing with polysemy or homonymy in a particular instance (Kuiper & Allan, 1996). Out of the 20 respondents, 11, which makes 55%, said that the word is homonym while 9, which gives us 45%, felt that it is a polyseme. Figure 4 below summarizes the above findings.

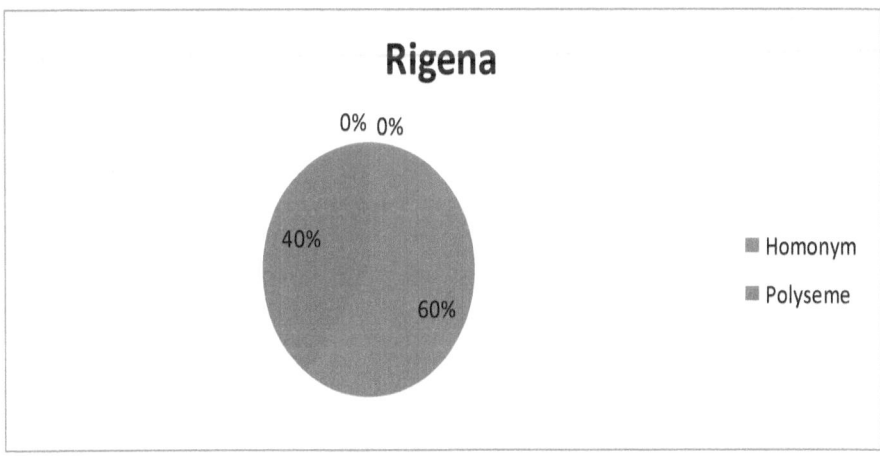

Fig. 4: Respondents' classification of *buruga*

Figure 4. shows that the majority of the respondents were in agreement that the word is a homonym but we over-ruled them because we felt that both involve an action of disturbing something that is still or settled. The action of weeding and stirring a liquid are almost similar. The core meaning is stirring a fluid substance and weeding is the derived meaning. The word therefore is polysemous.

The first distinction of distinguishing between homonymy and polysemy is relatedness or unrelatedness of the senses. If a word has two meanings which are unrelated, that word is a homonym. In Ekegusii, for example, the word 'egechege' refers to a wart and also to somebody naughty. The two senses are not related in any way. Alternatively, if a word has two related meanings, then it is a polyseme. To illustrate, the word 'omonene' in Ekegusii, refers to God which can be taken to be the central meaning. The other meaning is big. God is considered to be almighty. If a person is called 'omonene' he/she is being exalted like God. It also implies that the person is powerful in terms of wealth, body size and may be the mental abilities .The second meaning can be said to be an associated meaning or peripheral meanings. Lyons (1990) argues further that relatedness and unrelatedness is the only synchronically relevant consideration, which co – relates with native speaker's feelings that certain meanings are connected and others not The Ekegusii native speakers were able to use their intuitions about meaning in trying to distinguish between homonyms and polysemes, but still they were problematic.

The criterion of relatedness or unrelatedness, however, has been criticized. Lyons (1990) argues that the relatedness or unrelatedness of meaning may be a matter of degree. It may be demonstrated or not. There are cases where the intuitions of native speakers about relatedness of meaning differ. In Ekegusii, for example, the native speakers differed on whether to treat the word 'buruga' which means to stir and to weed as a polyseme or a homonym. The actions seem related but they are done on different things, stirring is done on liquids and weeding is a farming procedure. Another word that was controversial is engende which refers to either a bean or a clitoris. Some respondents felt that there was an obvious connection between them because of their shapes. Other respondents argued that there was no relationship between the two senses. They asserted that one is a cereal plant and the other is a body organ. We felt that the word is a polyseme because in Gusii land there were no beans. When they were eventually brought by the white man, the Abagusii might have noticed the close resemblance between their shape and that of the clitoris and given the former the same name as the latter.

The second mode of distinction between homonyms and polysemes is using the etymological information. This is the lexicographer's historical knowledge of the derivation of words. According to Lyons (1990), in the case of homonymy, the lexemes in question might have developed from what formally were distinct lexemes in some earlier stage of the language. This being a synchronic study, the researcher had very little etymological information about the Ekegusii words sampled since the language has no known etymological dictionary.

However, the researcher identified a few words classified as homonyms and polysemes which were borrowed from other languages and nativized. This is due to the interaction with other languages and also the spread of the new technology. In Ekegusii, for example, the word 'endege' refers to the central pole used in the construction of traditional huts or a plane .The second meaning came with the Europeans and nativized from the Kiswahili word 'ndege' meaning plane. Ekegusii, lacking a name for the plane, borrowed the Kiswahili word and made it endege meaning a plane, therefore, becoming a homonym.

Another word that is borrowed and associated with several related meanings is 'risasi'. The word is borrowed from the Kiswahili word risasi meaning a bullet .In Ekegusii, it has several related senses: it can mean batteries (e.g. for a radio, watch or camera), a bullet, a wise person and a male's reproductive cell (sperm). All the four senses have a conceptual connection of swiftness in movement.

Yet another distinction is the use of the test of ambiguity. This is where the different meanings implied are tested within one sentence; a co-ordination test may be employed. This test is used to identify homonyms in which case the meaning is manifest but, for polysemes, the meaning will cause confusion and be distorted. Consider the following:

Omonto orwarete amaru tarikonywa amaru.

Translated as, *a knee sufferer should not drink alcohol.*

Here, the two meanings for *amaru*, **alcohol** and **knees,** come out clearly and distinctively. It is believed that the Abagusii traditional brew, *amaru, has* a very strong effect on people who take it for it weakens the knees. *Amaru,* is thus a homonym. When it comes to polysemes, it is hard to determine the exact meaning implied by the statement. Here is an illustration.

Oborito bwagure

Oborito as discussed in below, can mean **something heavy** or **pregnancy.** *Bwagure* means it has fallen. Here this sentence is still ambiguous. It can mean, there is a miscarriage or something heavy has fallen.

One can also get the relationship between meanings by use of a metaphor, where a word appears to have both a literal and one or more transferred meanings. Intuitively, it is clear which the literal sense is. Such a word is a polyseme. In Ekegusii, for example, the word *'tuguta'* means to **throw away** or **bury**. The Ekegusii native speaker will use his/her intuitions about meaning and say that, **throw away**, is the literal meaning and **bury somebody** is the transferred meaning. Throwing something away means that the thing being thrown is useless. Likewise, the act of burying a dead person has the same implications because a corpse is of no value to the living. The two meanings have a connection of disassociating with a reject.

Homonymous and polysemous words in Ekegusii can be distinguished to some extent. The Ekegusii native speakers, using their intuitions, were able to identify words with multiple meanings and the relationships between them. This further proves that homonymy and polysemy in Ekegusii, which is part of the wider sense relations in lexical semantics, can be accounted for by the Sense Relations Theory because the notions of ambiguity and meaningfulness are explained in terms of sense Katz (2004).

In Ekegusii, we have some homonymous and polysemous words borrowed either from Kiswahili or English. In the case of homonymy, a word may be borrowed into Ekegusii but in the process of borrowing and nativizing it, it acquires another meaning similar to that of another word already in existence. A case in point is the word *ensa,* which means **a bundle of tied grass** and **a watch** or **time**. As explained earlier, the second meaning comes from a Kiswahili word *saa* which is nativized into Ekegusii. Therefore the word is homonymous. A word like *ekombiuta* is borrowed from the English word, **computer** to mean a machine and the brains. The word is polysemous because the computer is said to work like the brain.

The chapter observes that in Ekegusii, there are more polysemes than homonyms and that verbs tend to polysemy and nouns tend to homonymy. From the data collected, there are more polysemous verbs than any other group.

Conclusion

The chapter asserts that there are words with more than one meaning in Ekegusii. It has identified and explained words with more than one meaning in Ekegusii, drawn a distinction between them and shown that the Sense Relations Theory can largely account for homonymy and polysemy in Ekegusii. It has been confirmed that the two concepts are confusing, problematic and ambiguous.

In a nutshell, those studying local languages or developing dictionaries or dissemination materials like pamphlets, brochures among others ought to be aware of the lexical ambiguity inherent in any language such as Ekegusii. This chapter has shown that local languages besides official ones, as exemplified by the case study of lexical ambiguity in Ekegusii, are instrumental in re-engineering development so as to attain vision 2030.

References

Allen, K. (1986). *Linguistic Meaning*. London: Routeledge.

Central Bureau of Statistics Vol.1. (2009*). Kenya Population and Housing Census*. Nairobi, Kenya.

Cruse, D. A. (2000). *Aspects of the Micro Structure of Word Meaning*. Oxford: Oxford University Press.

Davis, S. & Gillion, S. B. (2004). *Semantics*. Oxford: Oxford University Press.

Fasold, R. & Connor-Linton, J. (2006). *An Introduction to Language and Linguistics*. Cambridge: Cambridge University Press.

Frath, P. (2002). *Polysemy, Homonymy and Reference*. France: *University* of Marc Bloch Unpublished PHD Thesis.

Gottlob, F. (1892). "Sense and Reference". Germany. *University of Jena Journal* Volume 19. Page 35.

Hirst, G. (1992). *Semantics Interpretation and the Resolution of Ambiguity*. Cambridge: Cambridge University Press.

Katz, J. (2004). *Sense, Reference and Philosophy*. Oxford: Oxford University Press.

Lobner, S. (2002). *Understanding Semantics*. Cambridge: Oxford University Press.

Lyons, J. (2005). *Semantics*. Cambridge: Cambridge University Press.

Pustejovsky, J. (1995). *The Generative Lexicon*. London: MIT Press.

Chapter Nine
Translation Constraints in Media Advertisements Translated to Ekegusii
Samuel Komenda and Colleta Maniga

Introduction

This chapter analyses the lexical, grammatical and rhetorical mismatches between English advertisements and their Ekegusii translations, and their effects on meaning and the effective translation strategies to be used. Ekegusii is an eastern Bantu language spoken by about 2.5 million people. About 2.2 million of these speakers are found in Kenya and about another 300,000 speak it in Tanzania. These speakers are distributed over Kisii and Nyamira counties, South of Kavirondo Gulf. The language is classified as central, E, Kuria (E.10). Ekegusii is closely related to Loogolia and Kuria and to the E.50 languages. Ten advertisements aired on FM radio stations broadcasting in English and Ekegusii were picked using purposive sampling procedures. Posters in health centres and administration offices were also sampled purposively for the analyses. The analyses have revealed that there exist lexical, grammatical and rhetorical mismatches between the advertisements rendered in English and those translated in Ekegusii. It has further been revealed that some of the mismatches led to loss of meaning whereas others did not. This occurred due to the fact that the translations were not carried out by professional translators but by the radio presenters, acting both as presenters and translators simultaneously. Effective translation strategies like paraphrase and target based translation should be used to overcome the above constraints. The researchers contend that the analysis done here will be important to media advertising companies and radio presenters who rely on translation to advertise various services and products. The researchers recommend that a study be carried out to establish the causes and strategies used in translation as a result of the mismatches noted.

Translation is the rendering of the meaning of a text into another language in the way that the author intended it to convey that meaning (Newmark, 1987). This means that translation should describe clearly the meaning of a text in the target language (TL) so that the reader can get the message that the author proposes. A good translation does not translate words but meaning. By translating meaning, the TL reader will be able to give an equal response to the message translated. This could be achieved by reproducing the message in as natural and accurate in the TL (Catford, 1965; Nida, 1974; Larson, 1984 and Baker, 1992).

Translation of texts entails a transfer of meaning from the source text (ST) to the target text (TT). A text has been treated in this article as a communicative occurrence that meets the seven standards of textuality: cohesion, coherence, intertextuality, intentionality, acceptability, situationality and informativity. If any of these standards is not satisfied, the text will not be communicative (Beaugrande, 1980). A text conveys textual meaning which refers to the way the text is organized as a piece of writing or speech (Eggins, 1994).

The presentation or interpretation of the sense of a text in one language and the production of another equivalent text in another language should establish a relationship of equivalence. Equivalence in translation is established on the basis of the linguistic and situational peculiarities of source and target texts, a comparison of the two texts and an assessment of their relative match.

In the process of translation, the translator is faced with various constraints. These include the rules of grammar of the source language, its writing conventions, its idioms and metaphors. The translator may also be faced with a problem of meaning transfer at the lexical, grammatical and rhetorical level. In this paper, it has been assumed that some mismatches are likely to lead to meaning loss.

Loss of meaning means that its transfer from the ST to the TT involves a certain degree of translation loss; that is, a TT will often lack certain culturally relevant features that are present in the ST especially if a text describes a situation that has elements peculiar to a natural environment, institutions and culture of its language area. This is because such peculiar areas that are brought about by culture-specifics can hardly be expressed in a different language for the lack of concepts and the way of speaking about them. Loss of meaning in TL texts, according to Bassnett (1991:30), results from language differences. Language differences usually results in untranslatability which inevitably leaves the translator with no choice but to pick a TL expression that has the closest meaning. In this paper, the various constraints translators face in the translation of English advertisements to Ekegusii and their effects on meaning loss or retention have been examined.

Scholarly works on translation have revolved around the major languages of the world like English, French, and German. In most African languages, there has been translation of literary works, but not much has been documented on translation in Ekegusii. To date, the Holy Bible and Christian Hymnals have remained as the only major translations and the only rich source of written Ekegusii until the recent publication of a translated dictionary of Ekegusii. Studies focusing on mismatches between ST and TT translation of advertisements and their effects on meaning loss are lacking, thus the motivation of this paper.

Advertising is a form of communication intended to persuade viewers or readers to take some action about a particular product. Different types of media can be used to deliver these messages. These include the use of traditional modes like newspapers, magazines, televisions, radios, outdoor or direct mail and modern advertising like the internet. Modern advertising has almost displaced the traditional modes of advertising. However, most advertising agencies still prefer to use the traditional modes of advertising because they have a wider reach of the populace compared to the internet.

In the recent past, globalization has led companies to communicate with consumers of diverse languages and cultures. Advertisements, therefore, need to be translated due to varying languages, literacy levels and cultural needs. Such factors are considered to limit the actual audience from receiving the message in the source language. Listening to adverts translated from English to Ekegusii in FM stations broadcasting in Ekegusii, [the native speaker no doubt notices a number of mismatches of the linguistic features between the ST and TT.

Mismatches between the ST and TT in a translation could occur because of cultural, grammatical, lexical and rhetorical differences between the two languages. This paper has examined these features in the hope of establishing any translation mismatches.

Translators in the framework of advertising should ask themselves the question of how to convey a single message written in two different languages, losing neither the spirit nor the identity. That is why translation is viewed not just as a straightforward operation performed on words, but as a translingual act of transcoding cultural materials (Howland, 2003).

In the case of translation of advertisements, the translator would have to be very sensitive to the losses of cultural elements. They should assess the "weight" (connotations, denotations and familiarity) of cultural elements in the source text in order to translate them into the TT and bring out the same effect in the ST.

The lexical, grammatical and rhetorical choices of advertisements are key to successful advertisements and their translations. In the process of translation, only when the linguistic characteristics are grasped, can the TT attain the purpose of the publicity.

Usually, advertising communicates information in three forms: audio, visual, and language. It is common for advertisement to have a mixture of the three. However, this study has limited itself to radio advertisements and their use of language. In radio advertisements, music is always accompanied by language. The current analyses have not focused on music. In most cases music provides limited information about the product and can lead to misunderstanding.

Methods

Population and sampling

The study population was drawn from advertisements aired on FM radio stations. Two sampling procedures: purposive sampling and random sampling were followed to draw data for the study. The researchers initially randomly collected advertisements from the FM radio stations.

Purposive sampling was used in the selection of ten advertisements restricted to lexical, rhetorical and grammatical feature analysis since they comprise the textual part of advertisements. These are the most important elements of the overall advertising message. The study focused on the lexical aspects like adjectival, adverbial and nominal usage. Focus was also placed on rhetorical aspects of advertisements like ellipsis and alliteration both in the ST and TT. Grammatically, the study focused on the types of sentences used in the advertisements in both the ST and TT. The researchers targeted advertisements with more than twenty words long as untranslatability tends to be higher in longer texts than in very short ones.

Advertisements were sampled from the fields of health, communication and education. These categories of advertisements are commercial in nature and are much more presented through the mass media. They, thus, were readily available to the researchers.

To arrive at the ten advertisements, stratified random sampling was used (Mutai, 2000). This was found effective as it ensured representativeness of the sample by ensuring that all the advertisements had an equal chance of being selected, thereby, avoiding any bias.

Research Instruments

An interview schedule was used to collect data for the analyses. At the same time, the researchers listened to aired advertisements. These were tape recorded to provide a back up to ensure the advertisements were captured accurately.

The interview schedule was used to collect data on the effective ways of translating advertisements from English to Ekegusii. The researchers used semi-structured questions where they presented the respondents with the advertisements both in the ST and TT and asked them to interpret them effectively. During the interviews, the researchers wrote down the responses, which were then analysed intuitively.

Data collection

In order to collect a variety of English and Ekegusii advertisements, the researcher listened to radio broadcasts in English like classic 105 and Easy FM and Ekegusii broadcasts in Egesa FM. The paper focused on English adverts since in the Kenyan situation, English is the business language and hence most adverts are initially written and broadcast in English. Egesa FM radio station was also preferred as it broadcasts mainly in Ekegusii and airs the translated English adverts. Radios were selected for the source of data as they have a wider reach and appeal to customers than the TV or print media thus satisfying the fundamental advertising axiom of reaching the right people, at the right time, with the right message.

Data Analysis and Presentation

The analyses done in this study focused on the textual part of the advertising message leaving aspects like music to future researchers interested in the acoustics of advertisements.

Content analysis was used to examine the intensity with which certain lexemes have been used in both the ST and TT. Creedon (1993) notes that, all advertisement texts have an underlying system of elements and rules that help produce their meaning. The elements examined in this study included an analysis of word classes, phrase structure, clausal aspects and their discourse functions. The words, phrases and clauses identified were classified to identify the lexical, rhetoric and grammatical mismatches in both the ST and TT.

Research Findings

The research findings presented in this paper have centred on the nature and presentation of mismatches in advertisements translated from English to Ekegusii and how the mismatches lead to meaning loss. The data are presented in words, phrases and clauses. Content analysis is used as shown in the example below:

1a AIDS has no cure. ..Prevention is possible

1b Enyamoreo tebwati riogo. Etange nenyamoreo botambe

An analysis of the advertisements above reveals the existence of a rhetorical mismatch in that there is the use of alliteration in 1a whereas

1b does not make use of alliteration. Instead the translator makes use of TT based translation where the source text's meaning is perceived then translated by use of paraphrase. The natures of the mismatches observed in the data collected are as discussed below.

The nature of the mismatches

The analyses of the data reveal the kind of mismatches in advertisements translated from English to Ekegusii presented below.

Lexico-grammatical mismatches

These are the grammatical properties of a word which typically determine the locations which the word can occupy in phrases or clauses. At the same time, they indicate the function which words have in phrases and clauses. The analyses of the data have revealed the existence of lexical and grammatical mismatches as the examples that follow indicate.

(a) Use of demonstratives

English demonstratives act as modifiers. They are of two monosyllabic forms: the one meaning 'this' or 'these' and the other meaning 'that' or 'those'. They are used attributively before nouns to show a sharp distinction in reference to proximity. In addition to proximity they indicate locations relative to the speaker or hearer. Consider the following examples:

2a... ***This Friday***

The Ekegusii translation of 2a was presented as:

2b... ***Ijumaa eye***   (Friday this) (back translation)

Similarly, there is a discrepancy in modification between 3a and 3b.

3a... ***This tariff***

3b... ***Etariff eye***   (Tariff this) (back translation)

(b) Use of pronominal reference

A text usually exhibits a variety of markers to show the relationship and distance between the sender and receiver. Mostly advertisements make use of pronominal variation and direct or indirect forms of address to establish the contact with the readers. It is important to note that language features denoting the relationship between the sender and receiver may differ between the two cultures.

In most cases, advertisers try to establish contact with the receiver in order to gain his or her trust and attention and persuade them on the necessity of the product or service. A characteristic feature of the English advertisements is the talking to the addressee in a direct user-friendly way as if engaging in a dialogue with the readers. This is reflected in the use of personal pronouns, especially the first person plural (we) and the second person singular or plural pronoun (you).

When the purveyor refers to the firm which offers certain products or services, usually the first person plural pronoun 'we' 'our' and 'us' are used. This creates the sense of informality and friendliness: the firm is presented not as impersonal, but as a personified body which helps to fulfill the needs of the reader. For example 4a and 4b have made use of the pronoun 'we' as shown below:

4a... *We aspire to serve.....*

4b...*Nigo totagete kobakorera*

(We want to serve) (Back translation)

Pronominal reference in the Ekegusii advertisements exhibits certain differences from the English ones. One of the possible reasons is that Ekegusii has verb tense distinction of the second person singular and plural. However, it is evident from the data that Ekegusii advertisements make use of two ways of reference to the audience: the first one is the use of the second person singular or plural pronouns. This is portrayed in 5 below:

5... *Buna okomenta chibesa ase esimi yao.*

(as you add money to phone yours)

      Where the prefix 'o' in *okomenta* 'to add,' means 'you'.

The other form of reference which brings a sharp contrast is the use of zero reference which portrays some form of informality between the sender and the receiver. The use of zero reference in the Ekegusii advertisements is signaled by imperatives where the addressee is implied. This is signaled by the use of verbs and the omission of the first and second person singular pronouns as portrayed below:

7... ***Aka esimi***   (Make a call)

8... ***Nyora freedom***   (Get freedom)

9... ***menta ekerediti***   (add credit)

10... ***Soa ase enetiwaki***   (Enter into the network)

Notably, there is a discrepancy between the English and Ekegusii advertisements as the latter makes high usage of zero reference when the advertisement does not directly address the audience. In such a case, the emphasis is seen to fall only on the advertised object and not the audience. The examples below further advance this observation:

11...Aka esimi yao ya Orange

(Make a call in your orange phone)

12... Menta ekerediti ase esimi yao ya safaricom

(Top up your safaricom mobile phone)

However, the above examples indicate that both English and Ekegusii advertisements make use of the pronoun 'you'. This tends to shorten the distance between the product or the producer and the consumer. It implies that the producer or the advertisement would be speaking to the consumer face to face, making sincere promises and honest recommendations. In so doing, the advertisement stands a better chance to move the receiver or customer to action, because the receiver feels that they are being thought of and taken care of and that they are the center point of the producers.

(c) Use of adverbs as modifiers

Another lexical discrepancy between the English and Ekegusii advertisements is on the use of adverbs as modifiers. Data exhibit a trend where most nouns in Ekegusii are post modified by the adverb 'yoka' (only) in singular and 'chioka' in plural. For example:

13...chisiringi isato chioka...

(Shillings three only)

The same is rendered in English as:

14...at three shillings per minute...

In the English advertisement the modifier is conspicuously absent. These adverbs are dominantly used in the Ekegusii advertisements and are aimed at appealing to the audience and making the message more persuasive.

(d) Use of adoption

Languages adopt new words primarily for concepts new to the culture of their speakers. The data reveals that Ekegusii has vastly borrowed new terminologies from English. Since Ekegusii lacks some technical terms, the advertisements have adopted some of them from English. Such words include; **SMS** for 'short text service', **promotion, pre-paid** and **post-paid, harsh** and **corporate banking.**

Rhetorical mismatches

More formally, a rhetorical figure occurs when an expression deviates from expectation, the expression is not rejected as nonsensical or faulty, the deviation occurs at the level of form rather than content, and the deviation conforms to a template that is invariant across a variety of content and contexts (Mcquarrier and Mirk, 1996). In order to realize the purpose of persuasion, advertising employs a lot of rhetorical devices. The following rhetorical mismatches were observed in the data.

(a) Ellipsis

From the data, 20 percent of the English advertisements made use of ellipsis. This is evident in the examples below.

15a.... *Switch today (to zain)*

15b... *Soa ase enetiwaki eye rero...*

(switch to this network today) (Back translation)

16a..... *that you have switched (to zain)*

16b....*Nga gwasoire ase enetiwaki enting'u*

(that you have switched to the strongest network) (Back translation)

Here the Ekegusii advertisements make use of reference instead of ellipsis. Equally 17 below employs ellipsis where the object 'of AIDS' is ellipted.

17a... *Prevention is possible*

There is, however a sharp contrast with the Ekegusii equivalent which does not employ ellipsis.

17b... *etange nenyamoreo botambe*

(Prevent yourself from AIDS always) (Back translation)

(b) Use of alliteration

One other feature evident in the English advertisements is the use of alliteration. This is the use of words that begin with the same sound in order to make a special communicative effect. Such words become pleasing to the ears because of the clever choice of words by the advertiser. In addition, the repetition of the beginning sound emphasizes the meaning the advertisement wants to express.

The English example below indicates the use of alliteration which lacks in their Ekegusii equivalents.

18a... *Freedom is finally here....*

18b... *igaa freedom nere aroro*

19a....*prevention is possible*

19b... *Etange nenyamoreo botambe*

20a ... *panadol provides a powerful pain relief...*

20b... *onye gokoromwa omobere....kanywe entetere ya panadol.*

From the above illustrations it emerges that alliteration is often not compensated for in the translations, but is merely ignored. Alliteration is very difficult to translate, as translators are expected to find words that both carry the same meaning in Ekegusii as they do in English and begin with a particular letter. In most cases translators adopt a free translation. The free translation ensures that it still functions as a persuasive device in the target language.

Effects of the mismatches

The paper has shown that in some cases the mismatches led to meaning loss whereas in other cases they did not affect the meaning of the advertisements. In cases where there was a mismatch in alliteration, there was no loss of meaning as the Ekegusii translation was rendered through paraphrase. Consider the following:

21a...freedom is finally here

21b...Igaa freedom nere aroro

(Here freedom is there) (backtranslation)

The above translation does not lead to meaning loss as the Ekegusii consumer can decipher its meaning.

The same is evident in the following translation:

22a... Panadol provides a powerful pain relief...

22b...onye gokoromwa omobere gose kobwate amaumibu....

(If you feel pain in the body or if you have pain) (backtranslation)

However, there are a few cases where the mismatches led to loss of meaning. This includes situations where there is the use of literal translation. This led to the mistranslations of the advertisements rendering them ineffective. This was noted in the written advertisements below:

23a... Identification of beneficiaries of deceased person's estates

23b... Kobaorokia ababwate enibo yomonto okure

(Identify those who possess the deceased's property) (back translation)

24a ... Burial certificate of the deceased

24b ... Ekadi yokoiborwa kwo monto okure

(Birth certificate of the deceased) (Back translation)

The above mistranslations could easily mislead the consumer as the meaning is completely distorted.

At the same time, it was noted that in cases where there was use of adoption as a translation strategy, there was a misunderstanding of the advertisements mostly to illiterate consumers.

Effective translation strategies

It was noted that most of the translation strategies used (adoption and literal translation) led to loss of meaning. The process of transfer of meaning through translation may lead to different results or different translations of the same text depending on the translator and the type of lexis in question. During translation, there are likely to be mismatches due to lack of equivalence. In order to examine the mismatches and how they affect meaning, a translation test was carried out. The test was carried out using the respondents. They were asked to effectively translate the advertisements from English to Ekegusii. The results of the respondents are presented in the table below:

English (st)	Ekegusii(tt) rendering	Respondent's rendering
Office of the president	Obisi yomorai bwense (office of the leader of the world)	Obisi yomorai omonene o'Kenya (Office of the leader of Kenya)
Burial certificate of the Deceased	Ekadi yokoiborwa kwomonto okure. (birth certificate of the deceased)	Ekadi yogokwa yo' Oyokure (Death certificate of the Deceased)
Identification of beneficiaries' Of deceased person's estates	kobaorokia ababwate enibo yomonto okure (To identify those who own the deseased's estates)	kobaorokia abagochia konyora enibo yomonto okure (To identify beneficiaries of the deceased's estates)
ATM card	ATM kadi	Ekadi yokorusia chibesa (withdrawal card)
Pre-paid and post-paid	pre-paid na post-paid	Baria bagoakana chibesa Bamanya goaka esimi Amo nabaria bagoaka Esimi bamanya goakana
Dial star one one	bata star eyemo eyemo	Bata eng'enang'eni Eyemo eyemo

The respondents noted that the most effective method of translation is Target Text (TT) based translation in which the translator gets the meaning of the English advertisement but uses another form to express it in Ekegusii or to say the advertisement in another form which conveys the same meaning. At the same time, they should ensure that the translated message must be equivalent to the dynamics of the original by communicating as much as possible, to the TL speakers the same meaning that was understood by the speakers of the SL, and evoke the same response as the ST. On the contrary, it was noted that this is not usually achieved in all cases since most of the technical terms are difficult to translate as there are no equivalents for them in Ekegusii. This led to doubts whether majority of the audience who happen to be illiterates get the intended message.

However, the respondents' translations revealed that the most effective translation strategy which can be used to translate the advertisements from English to Ekegusii is paraphrasing using unrelated words. This was effective because most of the SL items posing translation problems are not lexicalized in Ekegusii as evidenced from the analysis. Therefore, the translation was successfully done by unpacking the meaning of the source items.

Discussion of findings

Advertising language is often described as imitating spoken discourse. Goddard (2003:125) notes that spoken language is highly elliptical. In advertising ellipsis is used for language economy; also, it is used to create a sense of informality. In this paper, it was noted that some of the advertisements rendered in English make use of ellipsis though; this did not affect their meaning.

In most Bantu languages like Ekegusii pronominal association is expressed by the same morpheme /a/. This is why there is a sharp contrast in the modification of the noun in both languages. From the data it is very clear that in Ekegusii in the noun phrase, the adjective post-modifies the noun. In such a case, the noun agrees with the adjective by means of a prefix which in most cases is identical to that of the noun that precedes it. This is contrary to the English advertisements where the adjective pre-modifies the noun.

Shitemi (1990) argues that equivalence between ST and TT is affected by environmental, cultural differences as well as translation competence. In this paper it was realized that translation incompetence might have led to non- equivalence between the ST and TT and at the same time led to meaning loss. This was so because the translators were people working in the radio stations whose training might not be on translation. Perhaps no expert translators were engaged in the translations before they were aired.

Mutahi (1994) notes that during translation something gets lost. This loss arises due to the differences that exist between the two different languages which are both structural and cultural. The same observations were made in this paper; the loss was due to structural and cultural differences between the two languages.

Lobner (2002) asserts that an insurmountable problem for adequate translation can be posed by differences in social meaning. Expressions of meaning in Ekegusii, like most African languages, use much longer words than in English. That is, what an English word captures in just one word would require in most cases a phrase in Ekegusii. For example, in the advertisement on Trust Condom, in English the phrase is rendered as:

.... Use trust condom- (three words)

Whereas in Ekegusii it is rendered as:

....*tumia emepira ya trust condom* - (five words).

In the advertisement on the services offered by the chief's office, the headline in English is presented as:

Office of the president

The same is rendered in Ekegusii as:

Obisi y' omorai bwense

(Office of the leader of the world)

Here the lexeme **country** is mistranslated as **world**. Such terminologies that require phrases in the TL in order to translate them from the SL may influence and change meanings in the process of translation.

Conclusions

The analyses in this paper have shown that no matter what kind of structure, content or words used in the advertisement, all of them serve the purpose of attracting their audience by conveying information to them, and urging them to purchase the products or to use the service. That is what advertising is for irrespective of the language it is relayed in. Therefore, it is worthy to note that, irrespective of the myriad mismatches that exist between the advertisements most of them communicate the intended message effectively. On the other hand, there are some advertisements whose meaning is affected by the mismatches thereby, lowering the sales since the illiterate consumers cannot decipher the meaning. The research premise, thus, is that effective translation strategies like target language based translation and paraphrase can be employed to overcome the challenges of translation.

References

Baker, M. (1992). *In other words: a course book on translation.* New York: Routledge.

Beaugrande, R. de and W. Dresser (1980). *Introduction to text linguistics.* London: Longman.

Catford, J. (1965). *A Linguistics theory of translation*. Oxford: Oxford University Press.

Creedon, J. P (1993). *Women in mass communication*. London: SAGE Publication Ltd.

Eggins, S. (1994). *An introduction to systemic functional linguistics*. London: Pinter.

Gutt, E. A. (1991). *Translation and relevance: Cognition and context*. Oxford: Basil Blackwell.

Gutt, E. A. (1992). *Relevancy theory: A guide to successful communication in translation*. Dallas: Summer institute of Linguistics.

Howland, D. (2003). *The predicament of ideas in culture: Translation and histography*. Wesleyan University: Blackwell.

Larson, M. (1984). *Meaning based translation: A guide to cross language equivalence*. New York: University of America Inc.

Mutahi, K. (1994). "Translation problems in oral literature." *A Paper read at the Linguistic Conference of S.A.D.C.C. Universities* (LASU), Harare.

Mutai, B. K. (2000). *How to write quality research proposal: A complete and simplified recipe*. Nairobi: Thelley Publications.

Newmark, P. (1987). *Translation theory general remarks: Meaning and significance*. Hertfordshire: Prentice Hall International.

Nida E. A. (1974). *Towards a science of translation*. Leiden: E. J Brill.

Shitemi, N. L. (1990). "Mawasiliano katika tafsiri: Utenzi wa mtafsiri." *Unpublished M.A Thesis*. University of Nairobi: Kenya.

Notes on Contributors

Dr. Rachael Diang'a is an accomplished film critic and Lecturer of Film studies, Department of Film and Theatre Arts, Kenyatta University. Dr. Diang'a holds a PhD in Film studies from Kenyatta University. She has published articles/book chapters such as "Message films in Africa: A look into the past" (2016) and "Trans-formal Aesthetics and Cultural Impact on Sembene Ousmane's Explication of Xala" (2015) among many others. More importantly, Dr. Diang'a is the author of the first film book in Kenya entitled; *African Re-creation of Western Impressions: A Focus on the Kenyan Film* (2011). Her research interests are in Screenwriting, film production, film theory and Criticism, and Women in African Cinema.

Solomon Onchoke Aunga is an adjunct member of faculty Mt. Kenya University, Kitale Campus. He holds a Master of Arts degree in Applied Linguistics from Kenyatta University and a Bachelor of Education (Arts) Degree from Moi University. He has a wealth of experience of many years of teaching English and Literature in Kenyan high schools. Currently, Mr. Aunga his pursuing his PhD studies in Southwest University, China. He has published a number of articles that have appeared in refereed journals both locally and internationally. His book, *The Nature of Homonumous and Polysemous Relations in Ekegusii: Ekegusii Lexical Semantics-Homonymy and Polysemy* was published in 2012. His research interests are in the area of Applied Linguistics.

Charles Kebaya teaches at the Departments of Literature, Film and Theatre Arts, Kenyatta University. He has authored articles such as *"Historicizing Kenyan Comedy" (2015)*, co-authored a number of articles such as *"Community Theatre and Development Practices in the Nyanza Region of Kenya (2015)*, "Power and Gendered Identities: *(Re)Configuring the Gendered Self in Kenyan Drama" (2013)* and co-editor of a book, African Drama and Theatre: A Criticism (2012). His book, *Federico Garcia Lorca's Subversive Theatre: A Case of Blood Wedding and Yerma*, was released in 2011. Kebaya is also the executive producer of a documentary *film, Drugnets (*2015). His research interests include Television Drama, Literature, Theatre Arts and Dramatic Criticism, Visual Arts and Popular Culture.

Dr. Gatitu Kiguru is a Lecturer, Department of English and Linguistics, Kenyatta University, Kericho Campus. He holds a PhD in PhD in Applied Linguistics from Kenyatta University. His PhD thesis is entitled; "A

Critical Discourse Analysis of Language Used in Selected Courts of Law in Kenya". He has published widely in the area Language translation and interpretation in the Court system.

Samwel Komenda is an adjunct member of faculty at both Rongo and Kisii Universities. He holds Master of Arts degree in English (Phonetics and Phonology) from Kenyatta University and a Bachelor of Education (arts) degree from Nairobi University. Currently, Mr. Komenda is pursuing his PhD studies at Nairobi University. He has co-published articles such "The Morphophonemics of Vowel Compensatory Lengthening in Ekegusii" (2013). His research interests are in the area of Phonetics and Phonology.

Dr. Macharia Mwangi is a writer, researcher and educationist with a vast hands-on experience in the preparation, implementation and evaluation of learning programs both at the secondary and university levels. He holds a PhD in Literature from the University of Nairobi. His PhD dissertation is entitled; "Publishing Outposts on the Kenyan Literary Landscape: A Critique of Busara, Mutiiri and Kwani?" He has published several short stories in various anthologies and a few critical works. He has taught Literature at Kahuhia Girls' and Alliance Boys' high schools, Daystar, Laikipia and Kenyatta universities. He has also been a national examiner in Literature with the Kenya National Examinations Council. Currently, he teaches Literature at Kenyatta University. His research Interests are in East African literature and popular culture.

Dr. Mugo Muhia teaches at Literature Department, Kenyatta University, Mombasa Campus. He holds a PhD in Literature from Egerton University. His PhD dissertation is entitled; "Towards Indigenous Poetics: Orality and Stylistic Nuances in Ngugi wa Thiong'o's Gikuyu Fiction". He has published articles that have appeared in several refereed and reputable journals such as "Choru wa Muiruri: Relections on the Kamirithu Experience" (2014) and "Reconfiguration of Oral Genres in Ngugi wa Thiong'o's *Caitaani Mutharaba-ini/Devil on the Cross"* (2013) among others. His research interests are in the postcolonial novel, orature and popular culture.

Colleta Maniga is an adjunct member of faculty at Kisii University. She holds Master of Arts degree in Linguistics from Kenyatta University and a Bachelor of Education (Arts) degree from Egerton University. Her Masters dissertation is entitled; "An analysis of textual meaning in advertisement translated from English to Ekegusii". She has published a number of articles that have appeared in refereed journals. Her research interests are in the area of Language and Translation.

Amateshe S. Margaret is an adjunct member of faculty at both Kenyatta and Machakos Universities. She holds Master of Arts degree in English and Linguistics and a Bachelor of Education (arts) degree in English and Literature, both from Kenyatta University. She has been a senior graduate teacher for over 21 years with the Teachers' Service Commission and she is Head of the English Department at her current station. *The child with down's syndrome and cerebral palsy: A case study on speech development and intervention techniques* was published in 2012. Her research interests border the intersections of health and language communication.

Eric C. Maritim is a graduate of Kenyatta University in Kenya, where he successfully pioneered the academic study of the classic and modern Japanese literary art at graduate level. He is also a seasoned scholar, with major interests on the development of the contemporary African novel and drama, an area he has been widely published in different journals, both regional and international. He is also a keen practitioner and critic on the development of the Afro-voice in the context of the proliferation of the internet technology.

Velma Muyela is an adjunct member of faculty at Nairobi University, Kikuyu Campus. She holds Master of Arts degree in Literature from Nairobi University and Bachelor of Education (arts) degree in French and Literature from Kenyatta University. She is a senior graduate teacher for over 15 years with the Teachers' Service Commission. Ms. Muyela has published widely in the area of French teaching practices and the intersections between French language teaching and translation. **Hilda Kebeya (Phd)** teaches at the Department of English & Linguistics, Kenyatta University. She has authored articles such as "Language and Ethnic identity: More Perspectives from Africa"(2012), co-authored a number of articles such as "The growth and use of Sheng in advertisements in selected businesses in Kenya" (2015). She has participated and presented papers in various conferences on Language and Education in Africa, Language Literacy, Curriculum Development and Multilingualism. Her research interests include Sociolinguistics, African Languages, Translation and Languages in Contact.

Dr. Catherine Waithera Ndung'u teaches English language and linguistics, Department of Humanities and Languages, Karatina University. Dr. Ndung'u is a researcher and educationist with hands-on experience in the preparation, implementation and evaluation of learning materials in English Language and Linguistics both at secondary and university levels. She holds a PhD in English Language Education from Moi University.

She has published a book; *Phonological Variation in Gikuyu Language: As spoken by Kamba Traders in Thika District* (2012) and several articles in refereed journals. Her research interests are in discourse analysis, and language and translation.

Dr. Pamela Ngugi teaches at the Department of Kiswahili & African Languages, Kenyatta University. She has published articles such as *"Fasihi ya watoto katika kutekeleza mahitaji ya motto Kisaikolojia" (2014)*, *"Tafsiri katika Fasihi ya Watoto: Mbinu na Mikakati" (2012)*, co-authored articles such as "Kiswahili Poetic Aesthetic: From the General Identities to the African Prodigy" (2012). She is an author of various books such as *Ujasiriwa Tito (2014) and Abida Avuka Barabara(2012)* among others. Her research interests are on Language, Culture and Children Literature studies.

Prof. Martin C. Njoroge is the current Deputy Vice Chancellor – Academic Affairs at Pan Africa Christian (PAC) University, Kenya. He is a former International Institute of Education Scholar Rescue Fund (IIE-SRF) fellow and previously worked as the Director of Confucius Institute and as a Senior Lecturer in the Department of English and Linguistics, Kenyatta University. Prof. Njoroge is co-editor of Multilingualism and Education in Africa: The State of the State of the Art in 2014. His chapters have appeared in over 10 books while his articles have appeared in several refereed and reputable journals such as Multilingual Education Journal, African Journal of Educational Linguistics, and Confucius Institute Journal among others. He is the editor-in-chief of the Pan Africa Christian University Journal of Social Sciences. He is also a peer reviewer for the Commission for University Education. Prof. Njoroge has conducted extensive research on many issues of Multilingual Education, and various other areas of English language and linguistics.

Prof. Oluoch Obura is a professor of Literature and Theatre, Kenyatta University. Prof. Obura has held a number of administrative positions in Kenyatta University such as Acting Deputy Vice Chancellor Academic, Dean School of Humanities and Social Sciences among others. He has published widely in the areas of Drama, Theatre and Oral Literature.

Dr. Emily Ogutu is a Senior Lecturer, Department of English and Linguistics, Kenyatta University. She holds a PhD in English from the University of Birmingham, U.K. Dr. Ogutu has published several articles that have appeared in refereed journals such as "Mother Tongue amidst Other languages: Playing Roles in the Classroom and Outside"(2006), and "Our Flora and Fauna in our Proverbs and Sayings – our Aesthetics in Discourse - our Wisdom" (2006) among many others. Additionally, she has co-authored a number of books such as *Africa wide Integrated English Form 3 Students Book* (2005), *Teaching and Administering in African Languages* (2008) (Eds), and Discourse Markers among Speakers of Kabras: Forms and Functions (2010). Her research interests are in Text Linguistics, Discourse Analysis, Language as Communication, African Languages as Medium of Instruction and Politeness in Language Use.

Dr. Waveney Olembo is a senior Lecturer, Department of Literature, Kenyatta University. She holds a Doctor of Arts degree from Idaho State University and Master of Arts in Education degree from Ball State University, both in the U.S.A. She is an accomplished and distinguished editor and author. Some of her publications include: *When the Sun Goes Down and Other Stories* (2010), *Integrated English,* Book I (1986), *The Music of Poetry* (1986) among others. Her research interests are in Poetry, Caribbean Literature and Comparative Literatures.

Dr. Miriam Osore teaches at the Department of Kiswahili & African Languages, Kenyatta University. She has published articles such as"Reconstructing Reality in the Kiswahili Novel: The Role of Dreams in Euphrase Kezilahabi and Said Ahmed Mohamed's Novels" (2011), translated works such as *Vita Vya Kukata Masikio (2011), Almasi (2011).* Her edited creative work, *Jua Linapotua na Hadithi Nyingine*, was released in 2011. She has served as an English–Kiswahili–English Conference interpreter in a number of international conferences such as 2nd, 3rd, 4th, 5th, 6th, & 7th Ordinary Sessions of the Pan African Parliament. Her research interests are on translation aesthetics.

www.ingramcontent.com/pod-product-compliance
Lightning Source LLC
Chambersburg PA
CBHW031834230426
43669CB00009B/1352